THE GARDEN, THE CURTAIN AND THE CROSS

SUNDAY SCHOOL LESSONS
Teaching material for 3-5s, 5-8s and 8-12s

The Garden, the Curtain and the Cross Sunday School Lessons

© The Good Book Company, 2022.

Lessons written by Lizzie Laferton. Prepare Your Heart sections and Tricky Questions written by Carl Laferton.

Published by:
The Good Book Company

thegoodbook.com | thegoodbook.co.uk
thegoodbook.com.au | thegoodbook.co.nz | thegoodbook.co.in

Where indicated (ICB), Scripture references are quoted from the International Children's Bible®, copyright ©1986, 1988, 1999, 2015 by Tommy Nelson. Used by permission.

Where indicated (NIV), Scripture references are taken from the Holy Bible, New International Version. Copyright © 2011 Biblica, Inc.TM. Used by permission.

Where indicated (NIRV), Scripture references are taken from the HOLY BIBLE, NEW INTERNATIONAL READER'S VERSION™. Copyright © 1995, 1996, 1998 by International Bible Society. Used by permission of Zondervan. All rights reserved.

All rights reserved. Except as may be permitted by the Copyright Act, no part of this publication may be reproduced in any form or by any means without prior permission from the publisher.

Elizabeth Laferton has asserted her right under the Copyright, Designs and Patents Act 1988 to be identified as author of this work.

Design by André Parker | Illustrations from *The Garden, the Curtain and the Cross* storybook by Catalina Echeverri

ISBN: 9781784987169 | Printed in Turkey

Contents

Introduction — 5

Session One: Life and the First Garden
- *Prepare Your Heart* — 11
- 3-5s — 12
- 5-12s — 14

Session Two: The Choice We've All Made
- *Prepare Your Heart* — 25
- 3-5s — 26
- 5-12s — 28

Session Three: A Curtain Says "Keep Out"
- *Prepare Your Heart* — 41
- 3-5s — 42
- 5-12s — 44

Session Four: A Curtain Says "Come In"
- *Prepare Your Heart* — 55
- 3-5s — 56
- 5-12s — 58

Session Five: The Choice We All Face
- *Prepare Your Heart* — 69
- 3-5s — 70
- 5-12s — 72

Session Six: Life and the Last Garden
- *Prepare Your Heart* — 83
- 3-5s — 84
- 5-12s — 86

Tricky Questions — 99

Introduction

Welcome to this journey from Genesis to Revelation!

In this six-lesson series for 3-12-year-olds, the children you teach will learn the story of God's presence with his people. The series follows the structure of the best-selling storybook *The Garden, the Curtain and the Cross* and is intended to help children to dig deeper into the Bible passages and truths that underpin it.

Each of the six sessions in the series includes:

- a "Prepare Your Heart" section, helping you to enjoy and apply the truths yourself, before you teach them to your children's group.

- a lesson plan for 3-5-year-olds.

- a lesson plan for 5-12-year-olds, with different Bible-time questions and activities signalled as being for "Younger Children" (approximately 5-7-year-olds) and "Older Children" (approximately 8-12-year-olds). These teach directly from the Bible to follow the overarching story of the Bible.

- free, downloadable PDFs containing the relevant Bible passages, questions, activity sheets and illustrations for you to use with your group, as well as downloads of all the illustrations from the storybook. (You will see the icon to the right wherever the session is talking about something that is included in the download.)

The lesson overviews below give more details on exactly what the lesson plans for the different age groups include.

We have put each lesson together in a way that means you can deliver it exactly as it's written: all activities, scripts, Bible studies, questions, links and prayers are provided for every session, as well as games and craft ideas. (Please note that you'll need a copy of the storybook for teaching a 3-5s group). If preparation time is pressing, or you are new to teaching children, we want to give as much support as possible. At the start of each session for 5-12s, we've also included an outline of the aims of each part of the session, making it easy for you to adapt things to suit your particular group. At the end of the book, we've suggested ways to answer some of the questions that might crop up in each of the sessions (see page 99).

ⓘ *Where you see a text marked in this way in the 5-12s' plan, it's a note for you as the leader, rather than something intended to be read aloud to the group!*

Having bought this book, you now have access to free, downloadable material. You can download the content of this book as a PDF, for free, as many times as you like, to share with other leaders and helpers within your church. (Please note that you are not allowed to share it more widely than your own church.) You'll find all the downloadable material at **thegoodbook.com/gcclessonresources**, and will need to enter the passcode in the bottom right of this page.

L12MAB

At the back of this book, there's a list of "Tricky Questions" that each session might prompt, with some suggestions for how to begin answering them.

The scripts and Bible studies use the International Children's Bible (ICB), New International Reader's Version (NIRV) and New International Version (NIV). They will work with other translations, but we recommend aiming to use translations with simpler sentence structures, especially for the Bible studies where older children are being asked to find answers from the text themselves with less support. Memory verses are from the New International Version.

If You're Teaching 3-5-year-olds...

Session Structure

Each of the six lesson plans contains a number of segments that can be adapted for your circumstances.

The core elements of each lesson are:

1)*   A short opening prayer

2)   Reading the relevant pages from *The Garden, the Curtain and the Cross*

5)   A simple statement summarising that section's teaching (See the "God's Word Tells Us…" summary in each lesson plan)

6)   Sharing a Bible verse that shows that the truths in the book come from the Bible

7)   A simple closing prayer

* The numbers here correspond to numbered segments in the full lesson plans provided.

In addition, you can include any/all of the following optional elements:

3)   Simple questions that engage with the book reading

4)   A game that reinforces the teaching point as well as providing movement and a concentration break

8)   A craft activity that reinforces the teaching point

Sample explanations are also included for how to show the children the link between the game/craft and what they have been learning.

Series Overview

SESSION	MAIN TEACHING POINT
1. Life and the First Garden	It was wonderful to live in God's garden, and it was wonderful to live with him.

2. The Choice We've All Made	Adam and Eve decided they didn't want to listen to God. The Bible calls this "sin", and everyone sins. Sin means we can't live with God. The good news is: God has a plan to fix sin.
3. A Curtain Says "Keep Out!"	God's temple, and the "Keep Out" curtain in it, reminded people that it is wonderful to live with him, but because of their sin they couldn't come in.
4. A Curtain Says "Come In!"	God the Son came to live as a man called Jesus. Jesus died to take our sin. When he died, the curtain tore to show that Jesus had opened the way back to God.
5. The Choice We All Face	Jesus rose from the dead to live and rule as King for ever. Jesus invites us to be his friends and live with him for ever.
6. Life and the Last Garden	One day Jesus' friends will live with him for ever in a perfect world, where there won't be anything bad or sad. We will enjoying being with God, and we will say, "Thank you, Jesus!"

If You're Teaching 5-12-year-olds...

Session Structure

For each of the parts of the session outlined below, the lesson plans provide examples and ideas. Each full session plan also begins with an individual lesson outline going into more detail on the goals of each segment for that particular session.

With minor variations*, each session includes:

SESSION ELEMENT	PURPOSE
Introductory Activity	Introduce or set up an idea that will help the children understand the Bible ideas and/or apply the truths they will think about.
Recap	Provide a brief review of previous sessions.
Opening Prayer	Model prayer seeking God's help to understand and act on his word.

Bible-storytelling and Explaining	This first Bible teaching section is intended to be the briefer of the two (the sample scripts can be delivered at a slow pace in around 5 minutes). It involves the leader telling and explaining part or parts of the story of God's presence with his people.
Example scripts are provided that tell and explain the Bible story, using a mixture of paraphrased storytelling, Bible verses and explanation. The lesson plans also provide suggestions for how to engage the children visually or with movement in the storytelling.
Game	Different ideas are given for games that allow an opportunity to move about / take a break in concentration, but which also reinforce or set up a teaching point.
Bible Study and Discussion	This second Bible-teaching section gives children an opportunity to listen to or read Scripture for themselves and think about what it is saying.
In each lesson there are two different suggested studies, one for younger and one for older children. If you have the full age range in your class, these could be done in separate groups before you come together for the "For everyone" section.
Studies for younger children do not require them to read and involve a variety of activities to help them engage with and understand the passage. Studies for older children require them to do more close textual work and articulate their understanding for themselves.
The age ranges suggested are just a guide, and you may want to modify or combine ideas for your particular children.
Application	Depending on the session, this will involve a very short talk from the teacher or whole-group discussion or pair work or an opportunity to think individually. The aim is to encourage the children to consider what difference the truths you have been learning about make to our lives today.
Prayer	Model or give opportunities for responding to God and his word in prayer. Various suggestions for what this might involve are given, ranging from very supported/scaffolded to more open times of prayer.
Craft/Activities	An opportunity to exercise some God-given creativity and enjoy a reminder of the lesson! Various suggestions are given, ranging from those requiring pen and paper to crafts that need some minimal resourcing to more time/resource-heavy and/or complex projects.
At Home	Encourage families to keep thinking and praying together during the week about what the children have learnt at church. Suggestions are given for resources and ideas that could be shared with parents.

* The introductory discussion, recap and opening prayer may vary in order from lesson to lesson depending on which best leads into the first Bible-teaching section. In Session 4 there is an additional storytelling element after the Bible study, to dramatise the climactic tearing of the temple curtain.

Series Overview

SESSION	GOD'S WORD TELLS US...	SO WHAT?	BIBLE PASSAGES
1. Life and the First Garden	It was wonderful to live in God's garden, and it was wonderful to live with him. God's design for humanity is to enjoy living in his presence.	Knowing and enjoying God is what we are made for. Let's praise him for his creation and ask him to teach us that knowing him is the best thing about living in this world.	Talk: Genesis 2 v 8-10 Study: Genesis 2 v 7-9,15-16, 19, 22; 3 v 8
2. The Choice We've All Made	Like Adam and Eve, we all sin. Our failure to love and obey God means we cannot live with him. And it spoils life now too. We can't solve the problem of sin.	When we realise we sin, and that sin spoils our friendship with God and spoils life now, we can say sorry. And we can remember the good news that God has promised to fix the problem of sin.	Talk: Genesis 2 v 17; 3 v 1-6, 8, 22-24 Study: Romans 3 v 9-18, 23
3. A Curtain Says "Keep Out!"	God is committed to being with his people. In the Old Testament, repeated sacrifices made it possible for the sinless God to live among sinful people. But the temple "Keep Out" curtain was a reminder that people were still separated from God.	God didn't turn his back on people even after people turned their back on him. Let's praise him for everything this shows us about his loving character.	Talk: Genesis – 1 Kings Study: Leviticus 15 v 5, 7-10, 15-22

4. A Curtain Says "Come In!"	Jesus is God himself. God came to live among people as a man. Not only did God come to live among people as a man; he also came to make the way for people to know him and live with him for ever.	Jesus' death on the cross is a history-changing, life-altering moment. It deserves our attention and praise.	Talk: Matthew 1 v 23; John 1 v 14; 1 Peter 2 v 22; John 14 v 6 Study: Romans 3 v 23-25 Talk: selected verses from Mark 15 v 25-38
5. The Choice We All Face	Jesus rose from the dead! This means he has dealt with the problem of sin and death, and can offer his friends life for ever with him.	Jesus' resurrection means everyone faces a choice of whether to accept that offer. Let's think hard about our own response.	Talk: Matthew 16 v 21 and selected verses from Luke 24 Study: Acts 2 v 22-24, 32-33, 36-38
6. Life and the Last Garden	God lives with his people now by his Holy Spirit. One day God's people will live with him for ever in perfect relationship in a perfect world.	We have a LOT to praise God for now and a LOT to look forward to!	Talk: Acts 1 v 4, 8; John 16 v 7; Acts 2v 2-4, 38-39; Matthew 28 v 20… and many New Testament verses about the role of the Holy Spirit! Study: Revelation 21 v 1-5 and 22 v 1-5

SESSION 1
Life and the First Garden – Prepare Your Heart

 Read Genesis 1 v 1-31

- What does this chapter tell us about the nature and character of God?
- What aspect of his creative work most inspires awe in you?

The first sentence of the Bible introduces us to the basic reality that is the foundation of the universe, and of how we should view everything in the universe: "In the beginning, God created the heavens and the earth" (Genesis 1 v 1). God is the uncreated, eternal Creator of everything that isn't him. And, through his powerful word, he created everything out of nothing (Genesis 1 v 2-3)—the first chapter of Genesis displays an amazing Creator creating order, variety, and beauty from nothingness and chaos. He didn't have to make such a glorious variety of birds and trees, using such a glorious spectrum of colours—but he did!

The world in which we live, then, is to be enjoyed, and its Maker is to be praised. In heaven, right now, people are praising God around his throne, saying, "You are worthy, our Lord and God, to receive glory and honour and power, for you created all things, and by your will they were created and have their being" (Revelation 4 v 11). Today, try to take a moment to marvel at an aspect of creation—perhaps something as simple as a cloud or a leaf or a worm. And then take another moment to marvel even more at the one who first imagined that aspect of creation, and then created it with a word.

And then consider that the climax of creation is not the mountains or the stars or the lion but you and me—for it was only humans of whom God said, "Let us make mankind in our image, in our likeness" (Genesis 1 v 26). What does it mean to be made in his image? The first humans were to rule under him (Genesis 1 v 28). They had the role of extending the perfect Garden of Eden and of filling it with his image-bearers (Genesis 1 v 28; 2 v 15). And they had the joy of relating to him—to be like him, and to know him, and to enjoy him as they lived with him, under his good rule in his good garden. The best thing about Eden was the presence of God himself. This is what humans were (and are) made for—as the 17th-century Westminster Shorter Catechism puts it, "Man's chief end is to glorify God, and to enjoy him for ever".

Of course, this is not the world we experience today. The story of the Bible—the story you will be exploring with your group of children over the next six sessions—is the story of God's presence—of how humanity lost the joy of life with him, and of how God went to the most astonishing lengths to bring them—us—back.

So, before you prepare to teach your group of children, prepare your own heart by reflecting on these great truths. When you look at anything in the natural world, you are looking at something that was made by our unimaginably powerful, creative, imaginative God. When you look in the mirror, you are looking at the climax of his creation—an divine-image bearer, whom God made to enjoy him for ever. And when you look at the cross you are looking at the greatest statement of all of how much God loves you—how far he was willing to go to bring you back to his presence and delight in you there for ever. It's as we realise how good God is that we desire more and more to draw close to him in prayer now and look forward more and more to life in his presence eternally.

- How might these truths change your view of yourself, and your worth?
- How can you make sure that today you actively look forward to life in God's perfect presence one day?

SESSION 1
Life and the First Garden

God's Word Tells Us...
It was wonderful to live in God's garden, and it was wonderful to live with him.

3-5 year-olds

 1. Pray
Let's talk to God before we read the story:

Dear God, please show us why your first garden was so good. Amen.

2. Listen
Read *The Garden, the Curtain and the Cross* storybook from the beginning up to and including the page spread that looks like this but not the final line: "But then, one day…" (because you won't look at the next part of the story until the next session).

To make the reading interactive, you could:

- after the first page, ask the children what they would love to find in a garden.
- on the page that looks like this, before reading the right-hand spread, invite the children to say what animals they can see. They could act out those animals or make their noises.
- ask what the biggest animal is that they can spot. Which is the smallest?
- ask which animals they would have included if they had drawn the pictures.
- ask what else they think looks fun about the garden.

 3. Thinking
- Who made the world, the garden and everything in it?
- Did God's good garden have anything bad or sad in it?
- Could Adam and Eve see God and speak to God and just enjoy being with God?

 4. Game
Musical Statues / Freeze Dance. Before you stop the music each time, tell the children what to freeze as, each time naming something from the illustration of the first garden: for example, a roaring lion, a tree, an elephant, or someone swimming/playing hide-and-seek. Be ready to show them what each might look like!

OR

"Corners." Put a picture in each corner of your space of something from the Garden of Eden: animals, trees, the first people, a crown representing God. The children dance to music and, when the music stops, choose a corner to run to. Have smaller versions of the pictures ready in a bag and pull one out at random, saying as you do, "God made (animals/trees/people)" or (when you pull out a crown picture) "Best of all, God was there!" If the children have chosen the corner that matches the picture you draw out, they are the winners for that round.

Then say:

"What a fun game! Just like our game, the garden was full of laughing and playing and smiling and fun. But the best thing about the garden was that God was there!"

5. Summary Statement
It was wonderful to live in God's garden, and it was wonderful to live with him.

 ### 6. Listen to God from the Bible
We know this because in Genesis 1 verse 31 the Bible tells us, "God looked at everything he had made, and it was very good." (ICB)

 ### 7. Pray
Let's talk to God again now:

Lord God, you made everything, and you made it very good. Wow! It must have been wonderful to live with you there. Amen.

 ### 8. Craft Ideas
- Give the children the colouring page from the activity book for them to add to/colour/decorate with animal and flower stickers or other materials.

- Use paint or ink pads to make fingerprints that can be turned into flowers, animals, birds or people. (Have some that you have already done, to show children what they might look like.)

- Make paper plate animals or cardboard tube trees or flowers. (There are lots of simple ideas for how to do these on the internet.)

- As the children enjoy crafting, talk about all the good things there were in the garden and remind them that the best thing of all was that God was there.

SESSION 1
Life and the First Garden

5-12 year-olds

God's Word Tells Us...
It was wonderful to live in God's garden and it was wonderful to live with him. God's design for humanity is to enjoy living in his presence.

So What?
Knowing and enjoying God is what we are made for. Let's praise him for his creation and ask him to teach us that knowing him is the best thing about living in this world.

SECTION	PURPOSE	SUGGESTED ACTIVITY
Let's Get Ready Introduction	Introduce the concept of good gardens and what makes spending time in them enjoyable—who and what is there with us.	Brief discussion of the children's answers to an opening question.
Opening prayer	Pray for the session.	
Let's Begin the Bible's Story Bible teaching	Show that the garden itself was wonderful by describing for the children life in the first garden as full of wonderful beauty and abundance, where the things that make life hard or unhappy now were absent.	Tell the story of what was in the first garden using Bible verses, interactive storytelling and a picture from a page spread in *The Garden, the Curtain and the Cross* storybook. An example of what this might involve is given below and can be adapted to suit your age group, your timings and/or your personal storytelling style! Note: This section is not the principal focus of the lesson and is intended to be a shorter Bible-teaching segment than the second one.

14

🏁	**Let's Play a Game**	Provide a break for concentration. Reinforce and celebrate some of the things in the garden that made life there great!	Two games options depending on time / space limitations.
👂	**Let's Hear from God** Bible teaching and discussion	Help the children to: • see from Scripture that God was THERE, present in the garden with his people. • see from Scripture that God was personally involved with the people. • conclude that God's design for his world involves humanity enjoying living in it WITH HIM.	Age-appropriate Bible study and discussion questions from Genesis 2 and 3. Can be done in smaller groups.
💬	**What Does This Mean for Us?** Application	Draw out WHY "it's wonderful to live with him!"	Brief talk from the front to the whole group.
🙏	**Let's Talk to God about That** Prayer	Give opportunities to pray with praise and thanksgiving and/or to express other responses to what the children have been thinking about.	A number of different options depending on the circumstances of the group.
🎨	**Let's Get Creative** Reinforcement	Enjoy an activity together that picks up on an element of the story, perhaps giving time for conversation with the children about what they think about what they've learned.	Craft activities: Various options requiring different levels of resourcing.
🏠	**At Home**	Provide ways for families to continue thinking together about the wonder of God's presence.	Various possible activities that pick up on or reinforce this session.

Let's Get Ready

… by thinking about the best garden or park you've ever been to.

- Can you think of a garden or park you enjoy? What is there in the garden/park that makes it so great? Who do you enjoy being there with?

We enjoy those parks or gardens for what they have in them and also who is there with us.

Well, you know, a VERY long time ago, right here in this world, there was a garden. The first garden. The best garden there's ever been. And today we're going to be thinking about what made it so amazing. As we start…

 Let's Pray

Creator God, please excite us today about your good garden and show us why it was so wonderful. Amen.

So, what was so good about this garden?

Let's Begin the Bible's Story

… as God tells us in the book of Genesis what there was in the first garden that made it so wonderful.

> ⓘ *As you summarise the story of God's presence with his people in his creation, to engage the children visually you could use the picture provided for this session that looks like this from The Garden, the Curtain and the Cross storybook (either by holding up the book or as a print-out/on a large screen using the download provided) to refer to as you read the verses in the script illustrating segment might sound like.*

In Genesis 2 v 8 we read that "the Lord God planted a garden in the East, in a place called Eden. He put the man he had formed in that garden." (ICB)

Look, there is that man, Adam, and he is enjoying a swim with Eve. Maybe he's just splashed her and is making a run for it! We know there was a river giving the garden all the water it needed for life because it tells us in verse 10.

We also know the garden was full of wildlife because we're told in verse 20 that God brought them all to Adam for him to name.

- Which animals do you recognise on this page?
- What's your favourite animal of all the animals God has made? OR What other creatures would you have included if you'd been the illustrator?

Let's read on…

Verse 9 tells us that "The Lord God caused every beautiful tree and every tree that was good for food to grow out of the ground". (ICB)

So we know that God filled the garden with beautiful trees. And he filled the garden with trees that gave the people good food to eat.

- Do you have a favourite flower or a favourite type of fruit or vegetable?

There's more! Listen out for an unusual-sounding tree as I keep reading verse 9…

"In the middle of the garden, God put the tree that gives life." (ICB)

This is a tree that we certainly won't find in our local park.

- What was unusual about the tree?
- Which tree in the picture do you think that it is?!

In God's good garden, the tree that gave life meant that there were no illnesses or accidents. There was no death. There was NOTHING to make life bad! There was NOTHING to make people sad!

The first reason the garden was so amazing was because God had filled it with LIFE—full, varied, beautiful, happy, perfect, forever life.

 Let's Play a Game

OPTION 1

… that helps us think of some of God's amazing creations.

> *This option is quick and easy to play, involves less physical contact, and also gets children thinking of gifts of creation they could praise and thank God for.*
>
> *Have a selection of natural-world categories that are appropriately broad/narrow depending on the age of the children (birds or birds of prey, animals or farmyard animals or jungle life, flowers or types of tree, birds of prey, reptiles, creatures with four legs, and so on). In a given amount of time, individuals or team members compete to name as many examples for that category as possible. Depending on how challenging or competitive you want to make this, you could set a number they have to name in the time you have given, or say they must all begin with a certain letter.*

OPTION 2

… that helps us remember what made life in the first garden so amazing.

> *This option gives the children an opportunity to move about and reinforces some of the teaching points from the opening Bible story.*

Music will play for you to dance or move around to. As I stop it each time, I will shout out what you have to freeze as, and we'll see who can freeze the quickest and be the stillest and possibly the funniest!

If I call out…

- "tree of life", you have to freeze with arms up like branches and with a huge smile, because the tree meant there was nothing bad or sad.
- "river", freeze in a swimming pose like Adam and Eve enjoying the garden in the picture.
- "animals", pick your favourite animal and freeze trying to look like it.
- "food", freeze as if you're eating something delicious.

Let's Hear from God

Listen carefully to this verse from Genesis 2 and tell me who was there in the garden we've just been thinking about.

"The Lord God used the rib from the man to make a woman. Then the Lord brought the woman to the man." (v 22, ICB)

- Who was there?

> *Depending on how they answer, you'll need to draw out that, as well as Adam and Eve, God himself was there—he was with them. He was the one who took the rib from Adam and made Eve from it. He was the one who brought Eve to Adam. He was not somewhere else arranging everything from afar. He was present and involved. Drawing out God's presence from this verse helps set up the following Bible-teaching section.*

We've already thought about what was in the garden that made it so amazing. Now we're going to think about who was in the garden and why that made it even more amazing.

For Younger Children

I am going to read some sentences from Genesis chapters 2 and 3. In those chapters we learn all about what happened when God made the first people.

Every time I read a sentence, I want you to decide if it is telling us about something God did FOR the first people or something he did WITH the first people.

If you think it's something he did FOR them—something he gave them or something he did to help them—hold up four fingers like this [demonstrate].

If you think it shows God being WITH the first people—something that shows he was right there in the garden just like they were—interlock your fingers like this [demonstrate interlocking your fingers].

Sometimes you might think there's more than one answer, and that's fine!

Let's practise.

What would you do if I said, "God created a river to water the land?"

FOR: He's providing something for the people.

What would you do if I said, "God brought a duck to Adam?"

WITH: He's there with Adam and the duck! And if you think the duck is a good gift, you might also say "FOR"!

What would you say if I said, "God brushed Adam's hair!"? WITH and FOR: He is doing something for Adam, and he can do it because he's there with Adam.

> ⓘ *The children don't have to get these right! And in many cases there are reasons for suggesting either possible answer. The aim is that they realise God is there and that he is involved. Discussing why they gave the answer they did (whether "right" or not) provides an opportunity to draw attention to and emphasise those facts.*
>
> *You may well choose not to read all of these verses, but include some verses that clearly signal both God's presence with his people and his relational involvement with his people.*

PASSAGE	ANSWER
Genesis 2 (ICB) ⁷ Then the Lord God took dust from the ground and formed man from it. The Lord breathed the breath of life into the man's nose. And the man became a living person.	BOTH WITH and FOR: He was giving life, he "took" and "breathed"—he was present and intimately involved.

⁸ Then the Lord God planted a garden in the East, in a place called Eden. He put the man he had formed in that garden. ⁹ The Lord God caused every beautiful tree and every tree that was good for food to grow out of the ground.	Arguably BOTH: His presence is implied by the verbs "planted" and "put". And he gave the garden as a place to live. FOR
¹⁵ The Lord God put the man in the garden of Eden to care for it and work it.	BOTH: God was giving the man a job to do, and he "put" the man there.
¹⁶ The Lord God commanded him, "You may eat the fruit from any tree in the garden. ¹⁷ But you must not eat the fruit from the tree which gives the knowledge of good and evil. If you ever eat fruit from that tree, you will die!"	BOTH: God was talking with Adam. God was giving him an instruction which was for his good.
¹⁹ From the ground God formed every wild animal and every bird in the sky. He brought them to the man so the man could name them.	BOTH: God brought the animals to Adam, so God was in Adam's presence; God gave Adam a job to do.
²² The Lord God used the rib from the man to make a woman. Then the Lord brought the woman to the man.	BOTH: God brought the woman to Adam so again God was in Adam's presence; God had been intimately involved in fashioning Eve, just as he was with Adam; God was making someone just right for Adam.
Genesis 3 ⁸ Then they heard the Lord God walking in the garden. This was during the cool part of the day.	WITH

Now I'm going to read out three sentences with two possible options each time. From what you've seen from Genesis 2 and 3, which option do you think is the right one for finishing the sentence? Once I've read each sentence, hold up one finger/arm if you think it was the first option that was right. Hold up two fingers/arms if you think it was the second.

- When Adam and Eve lived in the first garden, God was right there with them.
  OR
  When Adam and Eve lived in the first garden, God was a long way away from them.

- When Adam and Eve lived in the first garden, angels gave them everything they needed.
  OR
  When Adam and Eve lived in the first garden, God himself gave them everything they needed.

- When Adam and Eve lived in the first garden, God wanted them to walk and talk with him.
  OR

When Adam and Eve lived in the first garden, God wanted them to stay away from them. We have seen that God's good garden shows us that he wants people to enjoy living with him.

For Older Children

> *For this activity, you could divide the verses among the children and ask them to decide which group their assigned verse(s) falls into OR assign a focus below and ask them to pick out verses they think fall into that group. This activity could function as an independent activity or a whole-group discussion depending on who is in your group.*

Read the following verses: Genesis 2 v 7-9, 15-17, 19, 22; 3 v 8.

Pick out sentences that show God was there with Adam and later Eve (Hint: Look at the verbs. Which actions can you only do if you are there?)

Pick out sentences that show God doing things for Adam and Eve's good.

Pick out sentences that show God being personally involved with Adam and Eve.

PASSAGE	IDEAS THEY MAY PICK OUT
Genesis 2 (ICB) ⁷ Then the Lord God took dust from the ground and formed man from it. The Lord breathed the breath of life into the man's nose. And the man became a living person.	God was intimately involved in making mankind—his very breath gave life.
⁸ Then the Lord God planted a garden in the East, in a place called Eden. He put the man he had formed in that garden.	God's presence is suggested by the planting and the putting. He provided a home for Adam in the garden.
⁹ The Lord God caused every beautiful tree and every tree that was good for food to grow out of the ground.	God provided trees that both were beautiful and met the first people's need for food.
¹⁵ The Lord God put the man in the garden of Eden to care for it and work it.	God's presence is suggested by "put". He provided a role, or job, for Adam in the garden.
¹⁶ The Lord God commanded him, "You may eat the fruit from any tree in the garden. ¹⁷ But you must not eat the fruit from the tree which gives the knowledge of good and evil. If you ever eat fruit from that tree, you will die!"	God's presence is implied by his direct conversation with Adam. He gave a command that was for their good. He warned of them what would happen if they disobeyed.

¹⁹ From the ground God formed every wild animal and every bird in the sky. He brought them to the man so the man could name them.	God's presence is shown by the fact that he "brought" the animals to Adam "to see what he would name them" (NIV).
²² The Lord God used the rib from the man to make a woman. Then the Lord brought the woman to the man.	God's presence is again signalled by the word "brought". As with Adam, God was intimately, personally and directly involved in making the woman.
Genesis 3 ⁸ Then they heard the Lord God walking in the garden. This was during the cool part of the day.	This is the verse that perhaps most clearly points to God's presence with them in the garden. Children may know that directly after this verse the people hid from God and then spoke with him. (But that's for the next session!)

- If you had been Adam, seeing the result of God's mighty creative power all around you… seeing all his amazing gifts of food… watching as he brought you animals and the perfect person for you… and hearing him speak directly to you and knowing God himself was out there walking in the same garden as you… what do you suppose you might have thought, felt, or said?

- Based on what you've seen from Genesis today, how would you fill in the gaps in this sentence?

    God's design for his world involved _____ enjoying _____

    in it with _____.

💬 What Does This Mean for Us?

God being present with the first people and God being in relationship with the first people is right at the heart of Genesis 2. Genesis 2 shows us that, "It's wonderful to live with him!" Let's just think about that for a moment.

Close your eyes and:

- imagine riding a horse or swimming with a dolphin—and right there with you is the God who made the horse and designed the dolphin.
- imagine standing in an orchard full of the most delicious fruit trees—and right there, handing you your favourite fruit, is the one who made them grow.
- imagine getting up in the morning—and right there to greet you as you start your day is the one who knows what it will hold and how to live that day well.
- imagine walking through the most beautiful garden you've ever seen—and imagine that next to you, talking to you, is the one who put the stars in outer space.

Open your eyes! I have a hard time imagining it—but I like the sound of it! And that's what humans were made for. It is wonderful to live with him.

Let's Talk to God about That

Here are a number of possible ways of encouraging the children to turn what they have learnt about God's garden and God's presence into prayers of praise. They move loosely from most supported and least independent to most open and least scaffolded.

1. Quickly play a round of the naming game (Game Option 1, p 18) with just the category title "Things God made"! Begin a prayer of praise for the children and invite them to call out any of those gifts of God's creation they want to say thank you for. Close the prayer by thanking God that the best thing about his good garden was that he was right there with the first people.

2. On a whiteboard or a large piece of paper have simple pictures representing the different things that made life in the garden so wonderful—the actions from Game 2 on page 18 might help for ideas here, and for living in God's presence you could draw two stick people alongside a shining crown. Children can show they want to pray aloud and say thank you for one of those things by choosing a picture from the board that they want to say thank you for. You can close by giving thanks for anything they've left out.

3. Discuss how they might finish these prayer sentence-starters and invite them to use them to pray, or use their ideas to pray on their behalf.

- *Creator God, we think you're amazing because you filled the garden with…*

- *Life-giving God, we are amazed to think of your first garden, where there was nothing bad or sad like…*

- *Father God, we think it must have been amazing to live with you, and we thank you that you made humans to…*

4. Ask the children what has most struck them:

- *about God.*

- *about life in the first garden.*

Is there anything that has been new for them or hard to imagine, or that has puzzled or amazed them? What does it make them want to say to God now? Give them the opportunity to pray individually either in their head or aloud.

 Let's Get Creative

Minimal resources:

- You'll need paper and coloured pens/pencils. Children can draw what they imagine Eden was like, based on what they have read. You could chat with them about what they find exciting about it.

Resources you may have available:

- You'll need the activity book accompanying *The Garden, the Curtain and the Cross*: creation colouring page and/or fill the garden page and/or learn to draw a quagga page.

- You'll need paper squares. Find online instructions for how to make simple origami flowers, fruit and animals. Children could write on what they've made "It's wonderful to live with him!" or "Best of all, God was there!"
- You'll need cardboard tubes, coloured paper/pens and glue. Find online instructions for making cardboard trees and/or animals. On a cardboard tree of life children could write "Nothing bad and no one sad".

More of a project:

- A shoe-box Garden of Eden that they decorate and fill.
- Begin a whole-series project: if you have space, time, resources and inclination, you could set up a panorama of visual reminders of the whole story of God's presence in Scripture that *The Garden, the Curtain and the Cross* storybook walks through, based around the six sessions:

1 – A glorious garden with two people

2 – A "Keep Out" sign

3 – A tent/temple and a curtain

4 – A cross and a torn curtain

5 – An empty tomb and a "come in" invitation

6 – A glorious garden-city with many people

You might do this as leaders to reveal each week and leave it set up ready to add to each session. Or, if your session is long enough for you to commit to a time-consuming craft, you could involve the children in making it. In Session One they could make paper/cardboard animals, plants and so on, as well as two people made from clay/modelling putty to populate a garden backdrop that you provide. A crown could be used to represent God's presence.

At Home

If you'd like to suggest ways that families could enjoy continuing to think about the lesson in the week:

- For younger children: They could read *The Garden, the Curtain and the Cross* storybook together. Perhaps they could have take-home questions along the lines of, "Who and what made life in the garden so amazing?" or "What did you think sounded most exciting about the garden?"
- Families could play the naming game together at the end of each day with a different category and turn the names they come up with into prayers of praise and thanks.
- Encourage children to learn a memory verse with their family or carer that praises God as the Creator:

"You are worthy, our Lord and God,
to receive glory and honour and power,
for you created all things,
and by your will they were created
and have their being." (Revelation 4 v 11, NIV)

SESSION 2
The Choice We've All Made – Prepare Your Heart

 Read Genesis 3 v 1-24

- How does the first sin affect the way the people relate to God, and the way God relates to the people?
- From verses 8-24, which would you say is the *most* awful consequence of sin?

This is a beautiful world, but it is also a broken one. The doctrines of creation and sin uniquely explain what we see around us and within us—why it is that you and I are capable of great good and also great evil.

What is sin? It is to choose not to love God and not to obey him as King. It is to seek to create a world where we set the terms and demand that God fits in with them, rather than enjoying a world with him as our life-giving King. It is to listen to the lie that he is not good, and that we would be better off without him.

That's the lie that the first humans listened to, when Satan slithered into their world and into their hearts by whispering, "God knows that when you eat from [the tree God had told the humans not to] your eyes will be opened, and you will be like God" (Genesis 3 v 5). That tree represented God's rule, which was what guaranteed the goodness of the garden. In taking and eating from that tree, Adam and Eve were rejecting the presence of God as their loving King. They wanted the gifts of God without the rule or presence of God.

And that's impossible. The tragedy of humanity is that, in our sin, we forfeit what we most need—the presence of God. Sin caused the first humans to try to hide from God's sight (3 v 7-8). Sin distances us from God, and God distances sinners from himself. The perfect God will not allow imperfect people to live in his presence, and so "the Lord God banished [the first humans] from the Garden of Eden" (Genesis 3 v 23). There was no way back in:

"After he drove the man out, he placed on the east side of the Garden of Eden cherubim and a flaming sword flashing back and forth to guard the way to the tree of life", which had given humanity eternal life in God's presence (Genesis 3 v 24). Since then, humanity has spent millennia seeking to build heaven on earth, without God. Our instincts to make things better and to protest injustice are a sign both that we sense the world should be better than it is and that we've never managed to build it.

The Bible is clear that if you and I had been there that awful day, we would have made the same choice—read Romans 3 v 9-20. We have inherited the consequences of the first humans' sin, and we have inherited their propensity to sin.

The challenge for us, then, is to accept that we, and the children we teach, are not good people with a few flaws, but sinful people in our hearts; and that our greatest need is not therapy or education or resolve but to be rescued from our predicament.

So, before you prepare to teach the children, prepare your heart by confessing your sin. Be honest. Be specific. Avoid excuses or explanations. Simply come before the God in whose world we live, and against whose rule we naturally rebel, and confess. Only those who are willing to admit their sin are in a position to discover that there is a Saviour. "If we claim to be without sin, we deceive ourselves and the truth is not in us. If we confess our sins, he is faithful and just and will forgive us our sins and purify us from all unrighteousness" (1 John 1 v 8-9).

- How does this encourage you to ensure that repentance is a key part of your life?
- How does the truth that *all* are sinners affect how we view other people?

SESSION 2
The Choice We've All Made

3-5 year-olds

God's Word Tells Us...
Adam and Eve decided they didn't want to listen to God. The Bible calls this "sin", and everyone sins. Sin means we can't live with God. The good news is: God has a plan to fix sin.

1. Pray
Let's talk to God before we read the story:

Dear God, please teach us what sin means and why it matters. Amen.

2. Listen

Read *The Garden, the Curtain and the Cross* storybook from this page spread…

… up to and including the page spread that looks like this:

The focus of this session lies more on the reality of sin in our lives today than on the details of the Genesis 3 story of the snake and Adam and Eve. Therefore the ideas below for how to engage the children during the reading don't pick up on the first page of the reading.

- After reading that God "sent them outside" the garden and away from him, ask the children how the first people are feeling in that picture.

- "Look at the X shape those two swords are making. What does that cross shape tell us? You can't…?" ("… *come in*"). You could get the children to make "Keep Out" cross shapes by holding their arms up, crossed at the wrists.

- Having read the final page of the section, spend some time here to help the children recognise the reality of sin and its effects in their own lives. Ask them what they think is happening in each of those three illustrations. Have they ever seen someone snatch or break a toy? Have they ever seen someone cry because they are sad? Have they ever heard anyone say angry words? If appropriate, they could act out being sad or being angry.

3. Thinking

- Did Adam and Eve listen to God and do what he said?

- Were Adam and Eve allowed to live with God anymore?

- Does sin make things bad and sad today, too?

26

4. Game
Play "May We Come In?"

The children stand on one side of the space, with a leader standing in the middle of the space. The children ask, "[Name], may we come in?"

The leader replies, "You may come in if you [are wearing red/have a younger brother/are 4 years old/have a pet dog]" and so on. The children who are in that category race to the other side of the space. Then they return to the start for another round.

Then say:

"In that game, I told you whether you could come in or not. God said that only people who listened to him and loved him could come in to his wonderful garden. Adam and Eve didn't listen to him and love him. Because of their sin, they couldn't come in."

OR

If you want something sillier, give a leader a large but harmless "sword" to wield, such as a pool noodle, and station them as an angel (like the cherubim in Genesis 3:24). The children have to try to run from one designated space to the other without being hit with a sword and "kept out".

Then say:

"In that game, [name] was like one of the cherubim with the fiery sword, saying, "You can't come in". God said that only people who listened to him and loved him could come in to his wonderful garden. Adam and Eve didn't listen to him and love him. Because of their sin, they couldn't come in."

5. Summary Statement
Adam and Eve decided they didn't want to listen to God. The Bible calls this "sin", and everyone sins. Sin means we can't live with God. BUT the good news is: God had a plan to fix sin.

 ## 6. Listen to God from the Bible
We know this because in Romans chapter 3 verse 23 God says, "All people have sinned and are not good enough for God's glory" (ICB). That's not good news.

BUT Romans 1 verse 17 says, "The Good News shows how God makes people right with himself" (ICB). That's good news! God has a plan to fix the problem of sin.

 ## 7. Pray
Let's talk to God again now:

Lord God, we know we all sin and that sin spoils things. We're sorry. Thank you that you have a plan to fix the problem of sin and put things right. Amen.

 ## 8. Craft Ideas

- Have paper/card "X"s or "Keep Out" signs for the children to decorate with red finger paint or pieces of red paper.

- The children decorate two paper plates, drawing a happy face on one and a sad face on the other. Staple them together with a lolly/popsicle stick attached as a handle, in order to enable the children to turn it round. Discuss how life in the garden was wonderful (happy) until sin meant Adam and Eve had to leave (unhappy), and how sin spoils things now and means we can't be with God (unhappy), but God has a plan to fix things (happy).

SESSION 2

The Choice We've All Made

5-12 year-olds

God's Word Tells Us…
Like Adam and Eve, we all sin. Our failure to love and obey God means we cannot live with him. And it spoils life now too. We can't solve the problem of sin.

So What?
When we realise we sin, and that sin spoils our friendship with God and spoils life now, we can say sorry. And we can remember the good news that God has promised to deal with the problem of sin.

SECTION	PURPOSE	SUGGESTED ACTIVITY
Let's Get Ready Recap	Recap Session 1.	Brief summary sentence activity— different options according to reading ability.
Opening prayer	Pray for the session.	
Introduction	Introduce the concept of rules and consequences or of "Keep Out" signs.	Two possible introductory discussions are suggested— one requires more set-up.
Let's Continue the Bible's Story Bible teaching	Show that sin in the first garden involved a rejection of God, and his goodness and purposes, which showed itself in disobedience. Understand the effect of Adam and Eve's sin on their relationship and presence with God, as well as what life for them outside the garden would be like (though emphasising the former).	Tell and explain the story of the fall and its consequences for Adam and Eve, based on Genesis 3, touching on: • what sin involved. • sin's effects in terms of their relationships with one another and with God. A scripted example of what this might involve is given below, and can be adapted to suit your age group and/or timings and/or personal storytelling style. There are also suggestions for how to make the storytelling visually engaging or to involve movement.

			Note: The language used in the suggested script and storytelling ideas of "turning your back on God" is picked up again in Sessions
🏁	**Let's Play a Game**	Provide a break for concentration. Enact the idea that sin involves turning your back on God.	Quiz-style game with an option for incorporating dance or movement. Other games ideas are suggested.
👂	**Let's Hear from God** Bible teaching and discussion	Show that the Bible teaches that everyone is sinful and is deservedly shut out from God's presence. Help the children to recognise outworkings of sin from their own experience. Show the difference between sinful outworkings and actions and the sinful heart attitudes towards God that lie behind them. Establish the need for a solution to the problem of sin to restore humanity to God's presence. Encourage the children by showing that God has provided a solution to the problem of sin.	Age-appropriate Bible study and discussion questions from Romans 3. Can be done in smaller groups.
💬	**So What Does This Mean for Us?** Application	Give the children an opportunity to recognise sin in their own lives.	Brief talk from the front to the whole group.
🙏	**Let's Talk to God about That** Prayer	Give opportunities to acknowledge and say sorry for sin and to thank God for his solution.	A number of different options depending on the circumstances of the group.
🎨	**Let's Get Creative** Reinforcement	Enjoy an activity together that picks up on an element of the story, perhaps giving time for conversation with the children about what they think about what they've learned.	Craft activities: Various options requiring different levels of resourcing.
🏠	**At Home**	Provide ways for families to continue thinking together about the reality and impact of sin.	Various possible activities that pick up on and reinforce this session.

ⓘ *If possible, to help illustrate the main teaching points, set up your space with lovely cushioned zones for groups of children, perhaps even with appropriate snacks. Have one attractively comfortable-looking seat or zone that is markedly different and which is reserved for you as the teacher.*

As the children enter the space, tell them they can choose any of the cushioned zones to sit in as they do the recap activity and that they are welcome to help themselves to anything to eat—BUT they must not sit in the teacher's seat. If they do, they will be sent out of the cushioned spaces and have to stand to the side.

Then proceed to the recap activity below.

(For added drama, tell them that the consequence of sitting in your seat or zone will be to be sent out of the room entirely, and prime an adult helper to sit in your seat and suffer the consequences. Since this runs the risk of a child deciding to sit in your seat before your adult helper can(!), you may prefer to make the consequence you threaten one you can follow through on and still keep the child involved in the lesson!)

Reference can then be made to this opening set-up in the introductory activity below. An alternative starter discussion is also provided.

Let's Get Ready

… by looking back at what we learnt last week.

For readers or where you can ensure there is a reader in each group of children:

Can you find and arrange your group's words and phrases to help us remember what we saw from Genesis last week?

ⓘ *Have words and phrases up around the room, using different-coloured paper (or different-coloured writing) for different teams. Alternatively write the words and phrases on a whiteboard, in the wrong order, for the children to look at. Children have to hunt or look at the words and then help reconstruct a sentence/sentences that sum up the last session.*

Here are some suggested sentence-summaries based on the storybook The Garden, the Curtain and the Cross.

- In the first garden, everything was wonderful.
- There was nothing bad, ever. There was no one sad, ever.
- Best of all, God was there!
- People could see God, and speak to God, and just enjoy being with God.

ⓘ *For non-readers:*

Show them this picture from last lesson and ask:

What was good about God's first garden? *(Allow them to share everything that excited them about it and, if necessary, add that God gave them everything they needed, God gave them each other, there was nothing bad and no one sad.)*

What was the best thing of all about God's first garden? *(Allow them to share what they thought was best about it and, if necessary, say, "I think the best thing of all was that God was there! It was wonderful to live with him!")*

Let's Pray

Loving Creator God, please prepare our hearts and minds to hear and understand what happened next in your good garden and what that means for us today. Amen.

Let's Start

… by thinking about what happened as you came into the room. You were given a particular job to do; you were given team mates to help you; you were given a choice of lovely places to sit; and you were given one—just one—rule: don't sit in the teacher's place. That's not for you. If you sit in the teacher's place, you will certainly have to leave the comfort and the food.

- When you came in, why was it right that you listened to me and followed my instructions? *(Answers might include: the teacher is in charge, the teacher knows what the plan for the lesson is, the teacher had provided the lovely space and food.)*

- How is that a little bit like Adam and Eve's relationship with God? *(God made and gave them everything. He knew what was best. He was in charge. They should have listened to him. The two additional questions below might help draw out the answer if needed.)*

- What good things did we see that God had given them last week?

- Why would it be right for God to give them instructions / for them to listen to and follow God's instructions?

Today we're going to find out what happened after God gave the first people one "That's not for you" rule.

OR

- Can you think of some examples of places where you are not allowed to go—perhaps at school, or at church, or even at home.

- How do you know you can't go in? Why are you not allowed in?

Today we're going to come across the first ever "Keep Out" sign.

Let's Continue the Bible's Story

… as we find out what happened next in the first garden.

> ⓘ *As you tell the story of Genesis 3, explaining its significance as you go, here are some very basic suggestions for ways to engage the children visually or to give them opportunities to move about, and a script illustrating what this storytelling-and-explaining segment might sound like. (All the Bible quotes in this script are from the NIV translation.)*
>
> - *Use picture displays (hard copy or on a screen) to refer to as you tell the story.*
> - *Use props and/or helpers to act out the story, incorporating different voices for God and Satan.*
> - *Have two props or images representing God and Satan and place them directly opposite each other. Have the children stand and face the prop they are "hearing" from at that point in the story. They hear from God, then they hear from Satan, and they move accordingly. They are enacting the choice Adam and Eve faced. When you reach in the point in the story where Adam and Eve choose to disobey, have them sit down facing "Satan". Their backs are to God. Adam and Eve turned away from him.*

When we left Adam and Eve last time, they were enjoying living with God in the world he had made.

God had given them each other. He had given them a special job: to grow God's place throughout the world. And he had given them everything they needed for life. In Genesis 2 v 16 we read that he generously said, "You are free to eat from any tree in the garden". Imagine that! It's the best buffet ever!

God gave them a good garden and a good goal. And then he gave them one—just one—good rule. So in Genesis 2 v 17 we hear him say, "You must not eat from the tree of the knowledge of good and evil, for when you eat from it you will certainly die".

Did you hear what happened? God, who made everything and knows what's best, gave the people one instruction, and he did it for their good, so that they would not die.

BUT: But now we meet another character in our true story. It's Satan, who appears here as a snake.

The snake suggested to Eve that God had NOT really been generous: "Did God really say, 'You must not eat from any tree in the garden'?" he hissed in Genesis 3 v 1. Well, we know God didn't really say that!

The snake suggested that God had NOT really been truthful: *You will not certainly die if you eat that fruit,* he lied in verse 4.

The snake suggested that Eve would be missing out if she didn't eat the fruit from the tree of the knowledge of good and evil: in verse 5 he promised Eve, "You will be like God".

So Eve faced a choice. Would she listen to and obey the one who had made her? Would she be grateful to the God who had done everything for her good? We find out in Genesis 3 v 6:

"She took some [fruit] and ate it. She also gave some to her husband, who was with her, and he ate it."

Adam and Eve chose to disobey the one who had made them. Instead of being grateful to the one in charge, they acted as if they were in charge. They turned their backs on God.

And that choice changed everything.

Do you remember that we saw that Adam and Eve had been able to enjoy talking with God, walking with God, and being with God? That is what he had made them for!

Well, listen to what happened next as we pick up the story in verse 8:

"The man and his wife heard the sound of the LORD God as he was walking in the garden in the cool of the day, and they hid from the LORD among the trees of the garden."

These people, who had been able to walk and talk and live alongside the Creator of the universe, were now running and hiding from him. They were hiding from the one they were made by and made for.

But they couldn't hide what they had done. God knew. And straight away Adam blamed Eve and Eve blamed the snake. Not only was their relationship with God spoiled, or ruined; their relationship with one another was spoiled too.

God told them what would happen next, because of what they had chosen to do. Just as he had warned Adam, they would now die. They would no longer be allowed to "reach out [their] hand and take also from the tree of life and eat, and live for ever", it says in verse 22.

God warned them that life would often be difficult and painful; their world would now sometimes be bad and sad.

But, worst of all, God sent Adam and Eve away—away from the garden and away from him. Chapter 3 of Genesis finishes in verse 24 with these words: "After he drove the man out, he placed … angels [called cherubim*] and a flaming sword … to guard the way to the tree of life."

The people's disobedience towards God resulted in the first ever "Keep Out" sign. They had disobeyed. They had wanted to be in charge instead of God. That is what that the Bible calls sin. And sinful people cannot live with a sinless God.

It's as if God said, *Because of your sin, you can't come in*. Life lived in God's presence had come to an end.

What a sad place to pause! We'd better do something to cheer us up!

ⓘ *Note: Make sure that you mention the word cherubim. It is returned to in Session 3.*

 **Let's Play a Game**

> ⓘ *The following game reinforces the key idea that rejecting God and what is right has consequences, and that one consequence is banishment from God's presence and place. You could play the game as a straight quiz. If you want to up the energy levels, ask each question and then play music for the kids to dance or jump to while they decide their answer, and then they have to indicate their answer when the music stops.*
>
> *Other game options: If you want something sillier and less targeted, furnish a small number of children with a large but harmless "sword" (such as a pool noodle) to wield, and tell them that they are cherubim (angels). The other children have to try to run from one end of the space to the other without being hit with a sword. If you really want to underline the point of the passage, set up your space so that it's impossible for anyone to make it past!*
>
> *You might choose to play other games that tee up concepts in the later Bible section rather than reinforcing the first one. That might include some sort of impossible target game or trying to jump an impossible distance between two markers: in other words, games that involve all the children falling short of what is required!*

In this game you are going to face a choice. I will read a question and give you two possible answers. The first answer is represented by this end of the room. The second answer is represented by that [opposite] end of the room. When you are told to, or when the music stops, if you think the first answer is the correct answer, you turn your back on [point] that end. If you think the second answer is the correct one, you turn your back on [point] this end. But if you choose wrongly, you are out of the game! We'll have three practice rounds first…

> ⓘ *Use lots of phrases like "reject" and "turn your back" on as you play the game: for example, "Oh look, Sam and Winnie have rejected answer two" or "Daniel turned his back on the right answer, and now he's out of the game".*
>
> *For the practice rounds, everyone stays in the game even if they choose the wrong answer. After that, suggest that children who are out stand to the side and can join in with any dancing and show how they would have answered had they still been in the game by turning their back on the answer they would have rejected. If appropriate, have small rewards for anyone still in at the end of the game.*
>
> *Here are some questions you could use (with information taken from DKfindout.com). They are all about God's amazing creation. Two possible answers are given, with the correct one in bold. If you want to use questions on a different theme, ensure you give two plausible possible answers. You don't want the children to keep getting these correct and never experience the consequence of turning their back on the answer that is right!*

- Roughly how many trees are there on the planet? About 500 billion / **About 3 trillion**
- How tall is the Venezuelan waterfall Angel Falls? **979m/3212ft** / 1176m/3858ft
- What was the hottest weather ever recorded? **56.7 degrees Celsius/134 degrees Fahrenheit** / 53.9 degrees Celsius/129 degrees Fahrenheit
- How many miles/kilometres of nerves are there in the human body? 23 miles/37 kilometres / **37 miles/60 kilometres**

- What percentage of your body weight is made up of muscle? **40%** / 62%
- To the nearest thousand, how many taste buds does a person have on their tongue on average? 7,000 / **10,000**
- Roughly how many insects are there alive on earth for every human being? 20 million / **200 million**
- How many species of birds cannot fly? **40** / 13

Let's Hear from God

 Use the pictures provided for this session (either as print-outs or on a screen) that show sinful interactions and behaviours.

- What do you think is going on in each of these pictures?

We recognise what's happening in those pictures because we've come across those things in the world around us.

We don't have to look very hard at our world before we realise that life for us is not like it was in the first garden. People get hurt or hurt one another; life is sometimes bad and often sad.

So we have to ask ourselves why. If people were made to enjoy living with God in his perfect place, why aren't we with God in the garden? Why is life outside the garden sometimes bad and often sad?

We're going to turn to another bit of the Bible now, in the New Testament, as we think about the answer.

For Younger Children

We're going to hear from God as we read part of the book of Romans. In this bit, the writer, Paul, is explaining why a particular group of people shouldn't think they're better than anyone else.

I'm going to read to you some verses from Romans chapter 3. Do a thumbs down every time you hear "no one", "no" or "none". Point to one another every time you hear the word "all". Let's practise! No one! All! No one! All! No! None! All! Ready?

Paul writes in verses 9 to 12 and 18 that all people are the same:

"They are all guilty of sin. As the Scriptures say:

'There is no one without sin. None!

There is no one who understands.

There is no one who looks to God for help.

All have turned away …

They have no fear of or respect for God.'" (ICB)

Is the answer to each of these questions "none" (thumbs down) or "all" (point at one another)?

- According to what God says in Romans, how many people in the world turn away from God, in the same way that Adam and Eve did?
- According to what God says in Romans, how many people love and obey God perfectly, as Adam and Eve were designed to do?
- According to what God says in Romans, how many people in the world sin, like Adam and Eve did?

What a sad truth. And we can see it's true when we read some other verses Paul wrote in this chapter—verses 13-17. Let's look at these pictures again *(see note for leaders on page 35)*. Point to a picture whenever you hear something that sounds like it's describing what you can see in that picture:

"They use their tongues for telling lies.

Their words are like snake's poison [which means they do harm to others].

Their mouths are full of cursing and hate …

Everywhere they go they cause ruin and misery.

They don't know how to live in peace." (ICB)

Adam and Eve's sin broke their relationship with God and their relationship with one another. God tells us that we sin too, and what we see around us in this world tells us that we sin too. And our sin is a big problem, because it breaks our relationship with one another and, worst of all, it breaks our relationship with God.

God says to us the same thing he said to Adam and Eve: *Because of your sin, you can't come in.*

For Older Children

We're going to hear from God from a part of the Bible that God inspired someone called Paul to write. In this bit of his letter, Paul is explaining why a particular group of people shouldn't think they're better than anyone else.

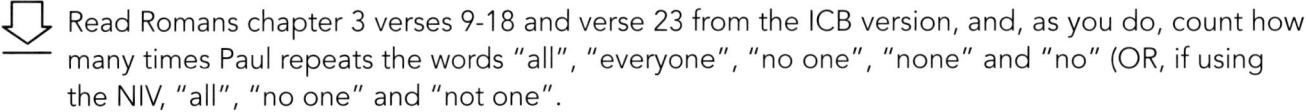

Read Romans chapter 3 verses 9-18 and verse 23 from the ICB version, and, as you do, count how many times Paul repeats the words "all", "everyone", "no one", "none" and "no" (OR, if using the NIV, "all", "no one" and "not one".

- What does Paul say is true about all humanity in verses 9, 10 and 23?

Read again verses 11, 12 and 18, in which Paul describes how people treat God.

- In what way did Adam and Eve turn away from God? How was their lack of awe of and respect for God's greatness shown?

Paul is describing how what was true of Adam and Eve is true of everyone.

- How would you put in your own words the attitude to God that Paul describes here?

In verses 13-17 we read about the effect of our sin on our lives and relationships.

- What examples of how sin looks, or its results, are mentioned in the passage?
- Which of the pictures that we looked at, and which we thought about in our own lives, are reflected in these verses (even if they are not quite as dramatic as these verses sound)?

Read 3 v 23 again. It tells us that our sin means that we are not good enough for, or fall short of, God's glory—that is, we do not live as God made us to, doing what God made us for, and so we cannot rightly claim we should be with God.

- What problem does that leave us all with, like Adam and Eve?

💬 What Does This Mean for Us?

Sinful people cannot live with a sinless God. So we face the same problem Adam and Eve faced: God says to us, *Because of your sin, you can't come in*. Instead of enjoying living with God, we find ourselves in a world where life is hard and death happens. That's not what we were made for. What a sad end to the story!

But, wonderfully, it's not the end of the story! In Romans 1 verse 17, Paul talks about some good news he wants to share with his readers. And, he writes, "The Good News shows how God makes people right with himself." (ICB)

We can't fix the problem of our sin to make a way back through the "Keep Out" sign to be with God again. But God can! And he has! It's what we will enjoy thinking about over the next four sessions. So, good news, everyone: there is GOOD NEWS to come!

But we have seen that what was true of Adam and Eve is true of us all, and we need to pause for a moment and think about that now.

I'm going to read some sentences that take the ideas of Romans 3 and put them in my own words. I don't want you to answer or say anything out loud. I just want you to think about them in your head, maybe with your eyes closed, remembering examples of when these sentences have been true of you this last week, or even today.

- All of us have said something that wasn't as kind or loving as it should have been.
- All of us have said something deliberately to upset or annoy or get back at someone else.
- All of us have said something that wasn't true, or wasn't the whole truth, or that bent the truth.
- All of us have shown anger or impatience or frustration to someone else by what we said or did.
- All of us have used our bodies in ways that weren't good for someone else.
- All of us have thought badly of someone else.
- All of us have chosen to argue rather than to make peace.
- All of us have made choices we knew God wouldn't like.
- All of us have lived at times as if loving God wasn't the most important thing to us.

When we all did those things, it showed our sin. We're going to pray now, which is a chance to tell God that we are sorry for our sin and to thank him that there is good news in the Bible about how he fixes the problem of our sin.

Let's Talk to God about That

Here are a number of possible ways of encouraging the children to turn what they have learned about sin and its consequences into prayers of confession and thanksgiving. You will need to judge what is appropriate for your group. They move loosely from most supported and least independent to most open and least scaffolded.

1. *Begin a "sorry" prayer and give the children a chance to say sorry to God in their own head if they want to. Close the prayer by thanking God for the good news that he has made a way to put things right again.*

2. *Discuss how the group might finish these prayer sentence-starters and then invite them to use them to pray (or use their ideas to pray on their behalf):*

   - *Holy God, we know that we sin by... We are sorry.*

   - *Perfect and fair God, we know that we do not deserve...*

   - *Merciful God, we thank you that there is good news. Thank you that you have...*

3. *Use the pictures from the "Let's Hear From God" section (page 35). Children could be given a picture to use in a corporate prayer that you begin with "Father God, we are sorry for the times when we..." and the children contribute to the prayer by saying aloud what is represented by the picture. (Or they could choose a picture that they particularly want to say sorry for.) Close the prayer yourself by giving thanks for the good news that God has made a way for people to be right with himself and asking God to prepare us to hear that good news.*

4. *Ask the children what has most struck them:*

   - *about sin.*

   - *about God.*

   - *about us.*

Is there anything that has been new for them or hard to hear, or that has puzzled or amazed them? What does it make them want to say to God now? Give them the opportunity to pray individually either in their head or aloud.

Let's Get Creative

Minimal resources:

- You'll need paper and coloured pens or pencils. Draw Adam and Eve having to leave the garden with cherubim warrior angels and the flaming sword guarding the entrance.

Resources you may have available:

- You'll need the activity book accompanying *The Garden, the Curtain and the Cross*: sin colouring page; wordsearch number 1.

- You'll need paper, water-soluble pens, water spray bottles. Children draw some sort of representation of the world (or of Eden or of themselves). Once they have finished (and having warned them this will happen), spray their picture with water from a bottle labelled "Sin". Sin spoils things and we can't undo it. Spray the children too! Sin affects everyone.

More of a project:

- Warrior angels: Add a face, silver foil armour or a paper robe, and wings to a cardboard tube, which you can then stand upright as a guard. Alternatively, they could make a flaming sword: stick red, orange and yellow tissue paper to a cardboard sword shape. Children could write, "Because of your sin, you can't come in" on one side or on the hilt of the sword.

- Whole series project (see this section in Session 1 for more detail on this): Add a visual reminder for Session 2, by getting children to work together on a giant collage "Keep Out" sign, sticking red paper squares onto the symbol/shape.

At Home

If you'd like to suggest ways that families could enjoy continuing to think about the lesson in the week:

- For younger children: They could read *The Garden, the Curtain and the Cross* storybook together. Perhaps they could have take-home questions along the lines of "Why did Adam and Eve listen to the snake instead of God?" and/or "What are some of the ways we use our words and our bodies in ways God doesn't like?"

- Suggest a simple game involving making a choice, such as Heads or Tails. (People place their hands either on their head or on their rear to show whether they think a coin will land on heads or tails. After the coin toss, anyone who made the correct prediction remains in the game, otherwise they are out. For a smaller number of people, play "How many did you guess right out of ten turns?".) Families could then discuss the choice Adam and Eve made and the choice we all make in rejecting God.

- Encourage children to learn a memory verse with their family or carer that speaks of the reality of sin:

    "All have sinned and fall short of the glory of God." (Romans 3 v 23, NIV)

SESSION 3
A Curtain Says "Keep Out" – Prepare Your Heart

📖 Read Exodus 25 v 1-9; 26 v 30-35

- What made the tabernacle more than just a tent?

- What links 26 v 31 with what happened when the first humans sinned? (Hint: Look at Genesis 3 v 24.)

God is determined not just to rescue a people but to bring them into his presence and blessing. God chose to make the family of Abraham, the Israelites, "my people" (Exodus 3 v 7, 10), as he told Moses, the man he would use to rescue them from slavery in Egypt. Though they would often forget it, the only thing the Israelites had going for them was that God had chosen to make them his people. All they had was him.

So it was that the most special tent in the Israelite camp, as they travelled through the wilderness towards the promised land, was the tabernacle—the tent where God dwelled among his people (which became the temple in Jerusalem). Inside it, the Israelites, enacting the instructions God had given them, placed echoes of Eden, for this was the place of God's presence and blessing. Just like Eden, it was made with gold and onyx (25 v 3-7; Genesis 2 v 12); and as Eden was full of beautiful trees, so the lampstand in the tabernacle looked like a tree (Exodus 25 v 31-39; Genesis 2 v 8-9).

But… this was a sinful people, as revealed by their repeated complaining about God and disobedience of God. The problem of sin had not been dealt with, and so, inside the tabernacle and around the Most Holy Place—the place where God dwelled in a way that was true of nowhere else in the whole earth—God told his people to "make a curtain … with cherubim woven into it by a skilled worker … [and] hang the curtain from the clasps and place the ark of the covenant law behind the curtain. The curtain will separate the Holy Place from the Most Holy Place" (Exodus 26 v 31, 33). This, again, was an echo of Eden—of the cherubim who God had put at its entrance, blocking the way into his presence so that sinners couldn't enter in (Genesis 3 v 24).

Only the high priest could go behind that curtain, only once a year, and then only after a sacrifice was made (Leviticus 16). The tabernacle told the Israelites that God's presence was the best place in the world, *and* that God's presence could not be enjoyed by people like them. The repeated sacrifices told them that God had made a way for him to be close to them, through the death of an animal in their place, bearing the consequences of their sins. Through the years, the curtain hung in the tabernacle, and then in the temple, saying, *This far, and no closer. This far, but keep out.* All the Israelites had was God, but God was still living at a distance from them. The best thing in the world was still something that was not theirs to enjoy. Only the greatest sacrifice, of the "Lamb of God, who takes away the sins of the world" (John 1 v 29), would change that.

So, before you prepare to teach your group, prepare your own heart by remembering that all you need is God. His presence with you is the most precious thing that you enjoy, and without him you could have everything this world offers but still have nothing. Ask yourself in what way you might be trusting other things—good things—in place of God, such that they, and not him, have become your security and your pleasure. Read Philippians 3 v 7-8 and reflect on what it would mean for you to echo Paul's words there, and say to God, "There's nothing this world can give me that I need more than you. You're all I have."

- What *would* it look like to echo Paul?

- Why is it better to be part of God's people today than it was back then?

SESSION 3
A Curtain Says "Keep Out"

3-5 year-olds

God's Word Tells Us...
God's temple, and the "Keep Out" curtain in it, reminded people that it is wonderful to live with him, but because of their sin they couldn't come in.

1. Pray
Let's talk to God before we read the story:

Dear God, please show us what the curtain in your Bible story was for and why it matters. Amen.

2. Listen
Read *The Garden, the Curtain and the Cross* storybook from this page spread…

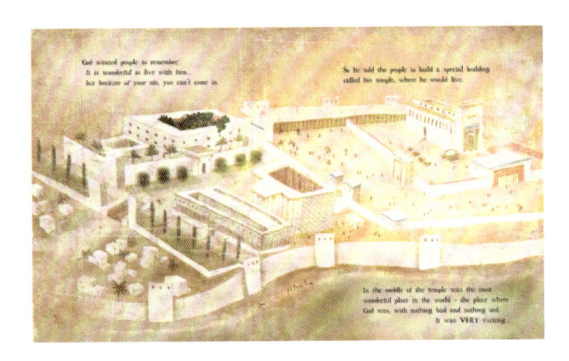

… up to and including the page spread that looks like this:

Here are a few ideas for how to make the reading interactive:

- Read the page below and point out the HUGE temple in the picture before telling the children that the next page will take them on a tour inside the temple.

- On the page below, *before* you read the text, ask the children what pictures they can see on the walls of the temple. Do they remind them of some pictures they've seen before in this book? You could show them the Eden illustrations and tell them that the pictures in the temple were to remind people of how wonderful it was to live with God in his good garden.

42

- On the same page, *before* you read the text, ask them if they recognise anything on the curtain. Where have they seen those warrior angels before? You could show them the picture of the warrior angels guarding the entrance to Eden earlier in the book, and the children could practise their crossed-arm "Keep Out" signs from Session 2.

3. Thinking
- Who came to live near people in a special building called the temple?
- When God told them to hang a big curtain, was he saying "Come in" or "Keep out"?
- Was sin still a problem?

4. Game
Set up some sort of course using foam tiles, cushions, hoops or something similar. The children have to step on them to get from one side of the room to the other. In some of the squares (or whatever you are using) put a red cross or a "Keep Out" sign, and explain to the children that they are not allowed to step in those places. Have fun stepping or jumping from space to space, taking care to avoid the "Keep Out" signs.

Then say:

"In that game, there were places you could go and places you couldn't. And in our true story, God's big 'Keep Out' curtain reminded the people that they still couldn't go where God was."

OR

Play "Red Light, Green Light" (in which the children start at the opposite end of your space to you, and are aiming to walk over and touch you, but can only move when your back is turned to them—if you turn round and see them moving, they must go back to the start)—but with a variation: if you hold up a red "X" or a "Keep Out" sign, everyone has to go back to the beginning.

Then say:

"In that game the "X"/'Keep Out' sign meant you couldn't come near. And in our true story, God's big 'Keep Out' curtain reminded the people that they still couldn't be where God was."

5. Summary Statement
God's temple and the "Keep Out" curtain in it reminded people that it is wonderful to live with him, but because of their sin they couldn't come in.

6. Listen to God from the Bible
We know this because in Exodus 26 verse 33, God gave this instruction: "Hang the curtain … This curtain will separate the Holy Place [part of the temple] from the Most Holy Place [the part where God was]" (ICB).

7. Pray
Let's talk to God again now:

Lord God, you came to live near people. Wow! But they still couldn't come in. We're looking forward to hearing how you got rid of the "Keep Out" sign. Amen.

8. Craft Ideas
- Decorate a rectangle made from coloured paper or card, or a small rectangular piece of cloth, as a curtain. Use pens, tissue paper, paint, gold glitter and so on. Encourage the children to include attempts at cherubim. Have red Xs or "Keep Out" signs drawn or printed on stickers for them to then stick in the middle of their finished curtain.

- For a quick resource option, use the "Keep Out" curtain colouring page from the activity book.

SESSION 3

A Curtain Says "Keep Out"

5-12 year-olds

God's Word Tells Us...
God is committed to being with his people. In the Old Testament, repeated sacrifices were the way he made it possible for him to live among sinful people. But the temple "Keep Out" curtain was a reminder that people were still separated from God.

So What?
God didn't turn his back on people even after people turned their back on him. Let's praise him for everything this shows us about his loving character.

SECTION	PURPOSE	SUGGESTED ACTIVITY
Let's Get Ready Recap	Recap Sessions 1 and 2.	Use pictures from *The Garden, The Curtain and The Cross* storybook to prompt children to remember the story so far.
Introduction	Set up the idea that God moved towards people despite their sin and was committed to restoring them to his presence.	"Run Away or Run Towards?" game.
Opening prayer	Pray for the session.	
Let's Continue the Bible's Story Bible teaching	Show that God was still committed to being present with people. However, humanity's sin meant people could only enjoy God's presence in a restricted way.	Tell and explain the story of God's presence among his people up to 1 Kings, drawing out that God remained committed to being present with his people but that this could not be as it had been in Eden. (For younger children, this might only focus on the tabernacle and the temple.) The tabernacle and temple curtain, with its woven cherubim, was a "Keep Out" sign that reminded people that they could not fully enjoy God's presence. For older children, you might want

			to fill in more of the picture between Genesis 3 and 1 Kings by touching on God's appearances to and presence with, for instance, Abraham, Isaac, Joseph and Moses. However, this is not the main focus and shouldn't take up too much time.
			See example script below.
			Note: The language used in the suggested script and storytelling ideas of "turning your back on" God from Session 2 is picked up in this session and will recur in Session 5.
🏁	**Let's Play a Game**	Provide a break for concentration. Intro the idea of swapping places.	"Change places If…" game or a team challenge involving swapping.
👂	**Let's Hear from God** Bible teaching and discussion	Establish that sin was a problem that needed dealing with for God to be present with his people. Show the swap involved in God's appointed way of dealing with the problem of sin. Prepare the children for next session's teaching on Jesus' substitutionary death for sin.	Age-appropriate Bible study and discussion questions from Leviticus 16. Can be done in smaller groups.
💬	**What Does This Mean for Us?** Application	Invite the children to consider God's activities in the Bible sections you have looked at, and what they show us about his character and priorities.	Open-ended discussion questions for use as a whole class or in smaller groups. Suggested questions are given on pages 52-53.
🙏	**Let's Talk to God about That** Prayer	Give opportunities to praise God for what you have seen about him in this session.	A number of different options depending on the circumstances of the group.
🎨	**Let's Get Creative** Reinforcement	Enjoy an activity together that picks up on an element of the story, perhaps giving time for discussing with the children what they think about what they've learned.	Craft activities: Various options requiring different levels of resourcing.
🏠	**At Home**	Provide ways for families to continue thinking together about God's commitment to his people and the "swap" pattern of dealing with sin.	Various possible activities that pick up on or reinforce this session.

Let's Get Ready

… by looking back at what we learnt last week.

I'm going to show you some pictures, and I'd like you to tell me what each one reminds us of from Genesis 1 – 3 and Romans 3.

> ⓘ *Use hard or soft copies of the images provided for this session as visual stimuli for this very quick recap activity.*

Let's Start

We're going to start with a quick activity called "Run Towards or Run Away?" I'll mention a thing or a person, and you have to show me if you'd run towards it or away from it.

> ⓘ *Depending on time and space limitations, you could have the children actually run away from or towards you to illustrate their answer. Otherwise they could point. The ideas below are suggestions, but if you use others, finish with relational examples that help illustrate the fact that, by and large, we keep our distance from those who hurt or wrong us.*

- an ice cream
- a bomb
- a gerbil
- a spider
- your best friend
- a Komodo dragon
- a rampaging elephant
- a much-loved family member
- a mean bully
- someone who has hurt you

There are lots of things that are dangerous, and so we have to keep away from them. Usually we enjoy being in the presence of those who love us, but we're less excited about being with people who don't love us. And normally, we move away from or avoid anyone who has done something wrong to us.

Today we're going to think about what God did next after he sent the first people—and all of us—away from his presence.

Let's Pray

Perfect, holy God, please amaze us today with how you treat people who sin against you and how you fix the problem of sin. Amen.

📖 Let's Continue the Bible's Story

> ⓘ As you summarise the story of God's presence among his people after Genesis 3 up to 1 Kings, here are some very basic suggestions for ways to engage the children visually or to give them opportunities to move about, and a script illustrating what this storytelling-and-explaining segment might sound like. Possible additions for older children in the script below are included in italics.
>
> - Use toy figures and props for Moses, the tabernacle/temple and the curtain, introducing each element at the appropriate point in the story. Have a "Keep Out" sign to stick onto whatever you use to represent the curtain.
>
> - Have two chairs with a word/picture on each to represent God on one and on the other humanity. Move them apart and turn them around as necessary to illustrate humanity turning their back on God, being sent away by God, then God NOT turning his back, and God moving towards (though not too close to) humanity again.
>
> - Have the children themselves sit on one side of the space with something representing God far over on the other side. When you share the verse about the tabernacle, move the prop representing God closer. You could overlay any picture/symbol representing God with a picture of a tent at this point. At the appropriate moment in your script, have the children move towards God but make them halt before they get too close (you could put down a taped line on the floor). If possible, hang a curtain to separate them from the prop representing God's presence at this point. (See also the note on page 54 at the end of the "Let's Get Creative" section about including a curtain ready for Session 4.)

From Genesis 3 we saw that sinful people can't live with a sinless God. It's as if God says, "Because of your sin you can't come in".

But living with God is what people are made for. It's wonderful to live with him. That's what Genesis 1 and 2 told us. So we have a big problem: it's wonderful to live with him, but our sin means that we can't.

Wonderfully, the rest of the Bible tells us what God has done to fix the problem of sin so that his people can live with him again. He didn't turn his back on people even after people turned their back on him.

We're going to think about what God did a long, long, long, long, super-long time ago because he hadn't turned his back on people.

> ⓘ Add the following sections (in italics) if you are telling the story with older children and/or if you have time in your session:

We're going to go on a super-speedy tour of some of the Old Testament stories now.

Strapped in and ready? Ok…

*Let's start with Genesis: you may have heard of Abraham and Isaac and Jacob? In various places in Genesis we read about God speaking to these men, and often we read the words "the L*ORD *appeared to [him]." God appeared to these men, made promises to these men and said he would be with these men. For instance, to Jacob he said, "I am with you, and I will protect you everywhere you go … I will not leave you until I have done what I have promised you" (Genesis 28 v 15, ICB).*

God didn't turn his back on people even after people turned their back on him.

Next stop, the second book of the Bible, Exodus.

God chose a man called Moses to rescue the people God had chosen out of Egypt and to lead them towards a land God had promised to give them.

Along the way, God told Moses to build a special tent. Here's what he said that tent was for. In Exodus 29 v 25-26, God says, "*I will live with* the people of Israel. I will be their God … They will know that I am the one who led them out of Egypt. I did this *so I could live with them*" (ICB, emphasis added).

Wow! God wanted to live with people again. The God who creates and provides and protects and is perfect still wanted to live with them! God hadn't turned his back on people even after people had turned their back on him.

But… this wouldn't be like Eden, where Adam and Eve could see and be with God—where they could walk and talk with God.

You see, in the special tent was an extra-special part where God would live. It was called the Most Holy Place. And separating this place from everywhere else was a HUGE curtain. Listen to this description of it from God's instructions to Moses in Exodus 26 v 31 and 33. God said:

"Make a curtain of blue, purple and scarlet yarn and finely twisted linen, *with cherubim woven into it* by a skilled worker. … The curtain will separate the Holy Place from the Most Holy Place" (NIV, emphasis added).

- What picture did you notice was woven into the curtain?
- Where have we heard about cherubim before?

The cherubim (or angels) on the curtain remind us of the cherubim guarding the entrance to Eden.

That curtain showed that although God was there with his people, they still couldn't be right with him, in his presence. It was a big "Keep Out" sign.

For older children/if you have time…

Now we are going to race through Leviticus, Numbers, Deuteronomy, Joshua, Judges, Ruth, 1 and 2 Samuel and stop, slightly breathless, at 1 Kings.

Many years had passed when God chose a man called Solomon to build a temple for God to replace the tent. It was a huge and beautiful temple, and it was full of things meant to remind the people of the Garden of Eden.

BUT, just like in the tabernacle, the special place in the temple where God lived was separated off by a huge curtain—the cherubim curtain, the "Keep Out" curtain.

The temple decorations reminded God's people that it is wonderful to live with him. But the curtain reminded them every day that because of their sin, they couldn't go in.

God hadn't turned his back on people even after people turned their back on him.

But sin meant things couldn't go back to being like they were in Eden either. What would God do about the problem of sin…?

And that's where we'll leave our story for now to come back to later.

🏁 Let's Play a Game

… that's going to get us thinking about swapping.

OPTION 1

> ⓘ *A familiar game that helps children let off some steam and involves changing places with others to tee up the idea of swapping/substitution in Leviticus 16.*
>
> *You need as many seats or spots as there are children, arranged in a circle with a leader in the middle. The game leader calls out, "Change places if you… [have red hair/are wearing green/go to x school/have a birthday in May, and so on]" and tries to steal the place of one of the children who are in the process of swapping. The person left without a seat then becomes the game leader and calls the next "Change places if…"*

OR

OPTION 2

> ⓘ *A game that can involve less physical contact if necessary and which incorporates the idea of swapping with someone who will accomplish what you can't.*
>
> *A points challenge game in which two teams compete to score points by successfully fulfilling an allotted task. Once they know the task, each team member can choose either to attempt the task themselves or to nominate someone on their team to swap with them.*
>
> *Successfully completing the task themselves: 5 points*
>
> *Trying and failing to complete the task: -3 points*
>
> *Nominated swap completes the task: 1 point*
>
> *Nominated swap fails task: 0 points*
>
> *Reinforce the idea by having the children say, "I need X to swap with me".*
>
> *You can come up with a variety of tasks, ensuring there are some that you know or suspect certain individuals can't do to help keep the swapping happening: for example, performing a gymnastics move, saying a sentence in a certain language, making a difficult shot.*

That game involved a lot of changing places / a lot of swapping with someone else who did what we couldn't.

We're going to think more about swapping now.

👂 Let's Hear from God

We have seen that God didn't turn his back on people even after people turned their back on God. But we've also seen that sin remained a problem. Even when God lived among them in the temple, sin meant that people couldn't enjoy God's unlimited presence. Sinful people cannot live with a sinless God. What was God going to do about the problem of sin?

We see the beginnings of the answer in the Old Testament book of Leviticus, as we read about a special event that took place at the tabernacle or temple every year.

For Younger Children

Our next true story took place in the special tent we thought about earlier. The main characters are:

- God
- Moses' brother, Aaron—God had given him a special job in God's special tent
- the people of Israel
- a bunch of different animals, including two goats

I'm going to read to you some of the verses from Leviticus chapter 16. Listen out for what happened to one of the goats and where the second goat ended up. What word beginning with the sound "s" do you hear over and over? (Assign questions to individuals if appropriate. You could use two toy or cardboard goats to help hold attention as you read the passage. One could be tipped over and one moved far away. You know the sensitivities of your group and how they will respond to the goats' fates!)

These are the instructions God gave for Aaron:

"Aaron must take from the people of Israel two male goats for a sin offering … Aaron must kill the [first] goat of the sin offering for the people … Aaron will [do this] to remove sins from himself and his family so they will belong to the Lord. Then he will remove the sins of all the people of Israel so they will belong to the Lord …

"Then he will bring the [second] goat alive to the Lord. He will put both his hands on the head of the living goat. Then he will confess all the sins and crimes of Israel over the goat. In this way Aaron will put the people's sins on the goat's head. Then he will send the goat away into the desert." (Leviticus 16 v 5, 15, 17, 20-21, ICB)

- What happened to the first goat? *(Died, killed, sacrificed)*
- What was removed when the first goat died? *(Sins)*
- Whose sins was the first goat dying for? *(Those of the people of Israel)*
- Where did the other goat end up? *(Far away, sent away, in the desert, in a lonely place)*
- Whose sins were put on the second goat before it was sent away? *(The people's)*
- So what was removed when the second goat was sent away? *(Sins)*

Let's play "Spot the Deliberate Mistake". You tell me which word I've got wrong in each of these sentences:

- To deal with the problem of salmon, God provided a swap for the people of Israel. (What word beginning with the sound "s" should I have said?)
- A goldfish died instead of them. (What word beginning with the sound "g" should I have said?)
- One goat swapped with them to pay the price for their sandwiches. (What word beginning with the sound "s" should I have said?)
- Another goat tucked away their sin. (What word beginning with the sound "t" should I have said?)

- Because one goat danced and the other carried sin instead of the people, God could live among the people. (What words beginning with the sounds "d" and "c" should I have said?)

Ok, let's hear what that should have sounded like:

To deal with the problem of sin, God provided a swap for the people of Israel. A goat died instead of them. One goat swapped with them to pay the price for their sin. Another goat took away their sin. Because one goat died and the other carried sin instead of the people, the people were able to have God living among them.

For Older Children

You're going to read parts of a passage in which God gave instructions for an event that took place at the tabernacle or temple which we thought about earlier. You will keep coming across the words "clean" and "unclean". This isn't talking about how much the people needed a shower. In Leviticus, the third book of the Bible, uncleanness has to do with sin. You might think of it as being spoiled by sin.

Read Leviticus 16 v 5, 7-10 and 15-22

> *For this complicated passage, the ICB or NIRV versions are helpful. Depending on which you choose, the text will use slightly different language as the translators have had to make choices about which aspects of the multifaceted words for "atonement" and "sin" to settle on. The questions below should work with either Bible translation, and the sample answers reflect the differences in translations.*
>
> *Depending on time and your group, you could assign particular questions (in bold below) to particular individuals ahead of reading the passage together. They could look out for those specific answers as they read the verses if this would be helpful to aid focus and/or build confidence with easier retrieval questions.*

QUESTIONS	POSSIBLE ANSWERS
What happened to the first goat in verse 15?	Killed/ sacrificed as a sin offering/for sin and death
According to Genesis 2 and 3, what was the price that humanity would pay for its sinful disobedience of God?	Death
So as the goat died, what swap was taking place?	The goat died instead of the people.
What happened to the second goat, according to verses 21 and 22, and what did it do?	The people's sins were confessed (admitted) over it and somehow those sins transferred to it before it was sent away. The goat carried away the people's sin.

Look again at verses 10 and 16. Which phrases tell us the problem that needed dealing with? What phrases tell us the purpose of this whole event? OR Look again at verses 10 and 16. In your own words, what was the reason for and the purpose of all the actions we read about in this passage?	Answers might include: sin and crimes, the people had been unclean/ were "not clean", had not obeyed; to deal with the problem of sin, remove sin, make things clean for God, make the place and the people clean (suitable for God), making it possible for unclean/sinful people to have God living among them (v16). Pay for the people's sins (v 10, NIRV) / remove the people's sins so that they will belong to the LORD
How would you finish this sentence? One goat died for sin, and one goat carried their sin away, meaning that God could…	For example: • live among them. • treat them as if they hadn't sinned. • live among sinful people.

💬 What Does This Mean for Us?

How could the sinless God live among sinful people? God's answer is a swap—a swap that meant a goat paid the price for their sin and a swap that meant a goat took their sin away.

BUT there was still a problem. Leviticus 16 v 34 tells us that God gave the instruction that the Israelites had to do this once a year EVERY year. The goats didn't get rid of sin for ever. Hundreds of summers and winters passed by. And sin was still a problem. So the "Keep Out" curtain stayed in the temple.

Would God do anything to deal with sin once and for all? Well, spoiler alert, the fact there are no nervous-looking goats hanging around at church this morning suggests the answer is yes.

But that's a true story for next time.

For now…

Let's think about what we have learned about God.

> *You could do this as a whole-group discussion or in smaller groups.*

Last time we realised that, like Adam and Eve, all humans ever since have naturally turned our backs on God. We enjoy his good gifts but ignore and disobey him.

- If someone treated you that way, how would you feel?

OR

- When someone does treat you badly, what words would you use to describe how you feel towards them?

This week we've seen that God didn't turn his back on people even after people turned their back on him. Do you remember our opening activity? Instead of running away from people, it's as though God ran towards them!

- What does that make you think about God? How would you describe him?

In Leviticus we've seen that God made a way for sinful people to be near him.

- Why is it good news that God chose to deal with the problem of sin?
- What does it show he cares about?

🙏 Let's Talk to God about That

… and use this opportunity to praise God for what we have seen about him today.

> ⓘ *Here are a number of possible ways of encouraging the children to turn into prayers of praise what they have learnt about God and his commitment to being present with his people. You will need to judge what is appropriate for your group. They move loosely from most supported and least independent to most open and least scaffolded.*
>
> 1. *Begin a prayer of praise for the children and invite them to call out any of the words they came up with to describe God. Close the prayer by thanking God for the fact that he is committed to being present with his people and for making a way to live with sinful people.*
>
> 2. *Discuss how they might finish these prayer sentence-starters and invite them to use them to pray, or use their ideas to pray on their behalf:*
>
>   - *Loving God, we praise you because when people turned their backs on you…*
>   - *Perfect and holy God, we praise you for making a way for…*
>   - *Wonderful God, we praise you because you are…*
>
> 3. *Use the pictures from the recap activity and also include the pictures provided for this session of the "Keep Out!" curtain and the goat. Invite the children to take a picture that makes them want to praise God or say "sorry" or "thank you" to him for what is illustrated in that picture. Open a time of prayer in which they can do that aloud or in their head.*
>
> 4. *Ask the children what has most struck them:*
>
>   - *about what God is like.*
>   - *about what God cares about.*
>   - *about how God treats people.*
>
> *Is there anything that has been new for them or has puzzled or amazed them? What does it make them want to say to God now? Give them the opportunity to pray individually either in their head or aloud.*

🎨 Let's Get Creative

Minimal resources:

- You'll need paper and coloured pens or pencils. Design the tabernacle/temple curtain and draw a sign for "Keep Out" (or write the words) on it.

Resources you may have available:

- You'll need the activity book accompanying *The Garden, the Curtain and the Cross*: "Keep Out" curtain design page; "Time Passes" drawing page.

- You'll need paper, lollipop/popsicle sticks, glue. There are lots of ideas online for different ways of crafting tents (2D on paper or 3D using easy materials or even origami). Make sure the children include a "Keep Out" curtain somewhere! Alternatively, take an A4/Letter-size piece of paper, turn it landscape, and draw a simple wilderness scene with a line parallel with the bottom edge, about an inch from that bottom edge, as the ground for the tabernacle to "stand" on. Take another square piece of paper to be the tabernacle, and cut a vertical line halfway up from halfway along the bottom edge. Fold the corners of the cut edge outwards, so that they look like tent flaps. Stick your square on the wilderness scene with the "tent flaps" open, with its bottom edge on the line you drew across the larger piece of paper. Children can colour the scene and the tent and draw or stick a "No Entry" or "Keep Out" sign in the gap inside the flaps.

More of a project:

- Weaving: Prepare simple looms made out of cardboard (instructions are readily available online) and provide wool or cloth strips for weaving a curtain.

- Whole series project (see this section in Session 1 for more detail on this): In this session children could help to put up a tent with you and hang a curtain and "Keep Out" sign at the entrance.

If you can make some sort of "Keep Out" curtain (complete with that message on it!) out of a sheet of some sort (or some real curtains), having this prop ready to tear dramatically in Session 4 would be a wonderful way of enacting that element of the story of the crucifixion.

At Home

If you'd like to suggest ways that families could enjoy continuing to think about the lesson in the week:

- For younger children: They could read *The Garden, the Curtain and the Cross* storybook together. Perhaps they could have take-home questions along the lines of "What did God do even though people had turned their backs on him?" or "What did the temple curtain show?"

- Suggest that families play any game that involves swapping cards, tokens, and so on (for example Happy Families/Go Fish), and then talk about how God provided the goats to swap with the people to take their sins away.

- Encourage children to learn a memory verse with their family or carer that speaks of God's mercy despite our sin:

> "He does not treat us as our sins deserve
> or repay us according to our iniquities."
> (Psalm 103 v 10, NIV)

SESSION 4
A Curtain Says "Come In" – Prepare Your Heart

📖 Read Mark 15 v 25-39

- What supernatural events accompany the death of God's Son?

- What does verse 34 imply about what was happening as Jesus hung on the cross?

The cross is the hinge of human history. Before then, the cherubim-embroidered curtain in the Jerusalem Temple served as a visual reminder that God's sin-marred image-bearers could not enjoy life in God's presence and instead faced the punishment of separation from him and all blessing and goodness. But on the cross, God himself took the punishment in place of his people—because on the cross, God the Son was separated from his Father's blessing, dying under his judgment, shut out from his presence. "God made him who had no sin to be sin for us, so that in him we might become the righteousness of God" (2 Corinthians 5 v 21).

Perhaps the most immediate and visual sign of what Jesus had achieved in his death was what happened a few hundred yards away from his cross, in the temple: "With a loud cry, Jesus breathed his last. The curtain of the temple was torn in two from top to bottom" (Mark 15 v 37-38). In an instant, the curtain that had kept humans out of God's presence in the temple was gone, because the judgment that would keep humans out of God's presence in heaven was gone. The direction of the tear signified that it was not that man had worked out a way back, but that God himself had done it all, ripping this thick cloth from the top. Here was the ultimate and final sacrifice, made once for all time, offering people a way through the curtain—the sacrifice not of an animal but of God's Son. We can now "enter the Most Holy Place by the blood of Jesus, by a new and living way opened for us through the curtain, that is, his body" (Hebrews 10 v 19-20). The cherubims' flaming swords have been placed back in their scabbards, and there is nothing between us and the presence of the one who made us to enjoy him for ever.

The cross, then, is the greatest statement of love the world has ever seen: that the Creator would humble himself to become a creature, and then die as a criminal, simply so that the creatures who had rejected his love and refused his rule could enjoy life with him. It is also the greatest statement of how committed God is to justice. He does not simply pretend our sin is not real, as though how we treat others and how we treat him does not matter; instead, he took the punishment mankind deserves on himself, as a man. Humanity has had its sin paid for through the death of the only human who did not deserve to die.

The cross humbles us. This is how far short of the glory of God we have fallen; this is what it took to restore us to him. The cross also lifts us: this is how far our glorious God was willing to go to bring us back to him.

So, before you prepare to teach your group, prepare your own heart by standing in your mind's eye at the cross. There is your sin. Here is what it deserves—death and separation from God's loving presence. Here is where it was dealt with—by another, in your place, loving you so much that he suffered his own judgment so you need never face it. Stand and look at the cross until you are ready, "in view of God's mercy, to offer your body as a living sacrifice, holy and pleasing to God" (Romans 12 v 1).

- Right now, do you need the cross to humble you, or to lift you up?

- The cross proclaims you are deeply, divinely *loved*. What difference could that make to you today?

SESSION 4
A Curtain Says "Come In"

3-5 year-olds

God's Word Tells Us...
God the Son came to live as a man called Jesus. Jesus died to take our sin. When he died, the temple curtain tore to show that Jesus had opened the way back to God.

1. Pray
Let's talk to God before we read the story:

Dear God, please show us why Jesus died on the cross and why that is good news. Amen.

2. Listen
Read *The Garden, the Curtain and the Cross* storybook from this page spread...

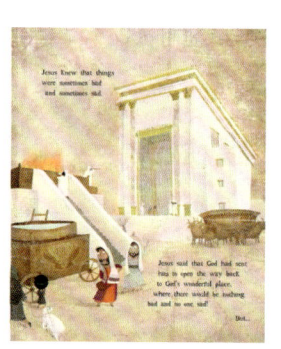

... up to and including the page spread that looks like this:

Here a few ideas for how to make the reading interactive:

- Read this page and ask the children why they think the person who drew the pictures chose dark colours.

- On this page, pick out a few of the pictures on the cross and ask the children what they think those pictures are showing. (You may need to help them with this.) Jesus died in our place to take the punishment from God for all those things.

- Give all of the children a piece of paper and invite them to tear it like the curtain (from top to bottom if they are old enough to have that level of dexterity) at the appropriate point in the story. What do they think those people in the picture of the temple curtain tearing are thinking and/or saying? They could act out the responses.

3. Thinking

- Who came to live on earth as a man called Jesus?
- Did Jesus die in our place to open the way back to God's wonderful place?
- Did God tear up the "Keep Out" curtain when Jesus died?

4. Game

Play "Swap Places"

The children sit in a circle. Each child in the circle is also given a picture or an object—this could be an animal, or a different coloured ball/brick, or anything that the children will recognise the name of. (Run through all the items before you start to check they know what each is.) Then a leader calls (for instance) "Elephant, swap places with lion", and those two children have to swap places. (If you need an easier option, you could just use the children's names: "Ryan, swap places with Melissa".)

If you have older children who could cope with a more complex version, have one chair/cushion fewer in the circle than there are children. One child stands in the middle of the circle. When two children swap, the child in the centre has to race to take one of their places. Whoever is left without anywhere to sit takes the place in the middle.

Then say:

"In that game, you swapped places with one another. Jesus swapped places with us when he died on the cross."

5. Summary statement

Jesus died to take our sin. When he died, the temple curtain tore to show Jesus had opened the way back to God.

6. Listen to God from the Bible

We know this because in 1 Peter 3 verse 18 God says to Jesus Christ's friends, "Christ himself died for you. And that one death paid for your sins. He was not guilty [he had not done anything wrong], but he died for those who are guilty [people who have done things wrong]. He did this to bring you all to God." (ICB)

7. Pray

Let's talk to God again now:

Lord Jesus, you died to swap with people and make a way back to God. Wow! Thank you, Jesus. You're amazing. Amen.

8. Craft ideas

- Pre-purchased or homemade cross crafts. An online search brings up various possibilities: scratch-art crosses; cross sun-catchers to colour in; wooden crosses to decorate with appropriate pens or stickers; lollypop/popsicle stick crosses to decorate; foam cross craft kits; fuzzy art crosses to colour in.

- Cut out multiple copies of print-outs of the pictures showing sinful behaviours/attitudes provided for this session. The children can glue them as a collage onto one side of a card cross. At the end of the activity, ask the children to turn the cross over onto the blank side. Jesus died to take our sin away at the cross. They could decorate that blank side with smiley faces.

SESSION 4

A Curtain Says "Come In"

5-12 year-olds

God's Word Tells Us...
Jesus is God himself. Not only did God come to live among people as a man, he also came to make the way for people to know him and live with him for ever.

So What?
Jesus' death on the cross is a history-changing, life-altering moment. It deserves our attention and our praise.

SECTION	PURPOSE	SUGGESTED ACTIVITY
Let's Get Ready Introduction	Introduce the idea of world-changing events ready for the discussion at the end.	Quick discussion activities (alternatives suggested for different age groups).
Opening prayer	Pray for the session	
Recap	Recap Sessions 1-3 to lead into the Bible storytelling segment that comes next.	Use the pictures provided for this session for an activity where the children have to arrange them in chronological order.
Let's Continue the Bible's Story Bible teaching	Summarise Jesus' identity and mission with a focus on him being God among us and making a way for people to be restored to being with God for ever.	Share with the children details of Jesus' birth, life and teachings that show them: • Jesus is God the Son, God himself, and he proved it through his life and deeds. Jesus was sinless. • Jesus brought God's presence among people. • Jesus came to make a way to return people to God's presence for ever. A scripted example of what this might involve is given on page 61 and can be adapted to suit your

			age group, timings and personal storytelling style. There are also suggestions for how to make the storytelling visually engaging or to involve movement.
🏁	**Let's Play a Game**	Provide a break for concentration. Introduce the idea of needing someone to rescue us *or* to show us the way.	Stuck in the Mud / Freeze Tag OR Minefield
👂	**Let's Hear from God** Bible teaching and discussion	Teach the mechanism and achievement of the cross, focusing mainly on the latter. Show that Jesus is the once-for-all sacrifice of atonement for sin. Encourage the children to recognise that a swap took place. Consider whose sins were being punished on the cross and how it relates to us.	Age-appropriate Bible study and discussion questions from Romans 3. Can be done in smaller groups. (This is a shorter study than in previous sessions to leave room for an extra, crucial Bible-storytelling segment on page 65, in which the curtain is torn.)
📖	**Let's Continue the Bible's Story** Bible teaching	Help the children appreciate the tearing of the temple curtain as climactic and history-changing. Emphasise that Jesus' death was a success: it made a way back, through the "Keep Out" sign, to being with God again.	Tell the story from Scripture of the temple curtain tearing at Jesus' death, using appropriate resources to reflect the climactic nature of that moment. A scripted example of what this might involve is given on page 65 and can be adapted to suit your group and style.
💬	**What Does This Mean for Us?** Application	Invite the children to consider why Jesus' death on the cross is such a history-changing moment.	Open-ended discussion as a whole class or in smaller groups. Suggested questions are given on pages 65-66.
🙏	**Let's Talk to God about That** Prayer	Give opportunities to praise God for what you have seen about him in this session.	A number of different options depending on your group circumstances.
🎨	**Let's Get Creative** Reinforcement	Enjoy an activity together that picks up on an element of the story, perhaps giving time for discussing with the children what they think about what they've learned.	Craft activities: Various options requiring different levels of resourcing.
🏠	**At Home**	Provide ways for families to continue thinking together about the wonder of the cross.	Various possible activities that pick up on or reinforce this session.

Let's Get Ready

For Younger Children

Choose five or six major events in human history that will be recognisable to the children in your group and find pictures to represent them. These might be, for instance, a key moment in your country's history; the first person in space; or a key invention such as the light bulb, television or the internet.

I'm going to show you some pictures, and then I'm going to tell you some things that have happened in the past that have made a huge change to the world and to us. I want you to try to work out which picture goes with which event.

Invite the children to identify which picture corresponds to which event and briefly articulate why that event was so impactful on human history.

For Older Children

In your pairs/groups, you have x minutes to choose three events from history, and not from the Bible, that you think have changed human life in a huge way. They can be from any century and any place.

Invite groups to feed back their events and why they thought those events had such an impact. If you are a large group, do this feedback in smaller sub-groups to keep the exercise brief.

Let's Pray

Lord God who rules history, please excite us about the life-changing event we are going to think about today. Amen.

Let's Look Back

Use the pictures provided for this session and invite the children to tell you which order they should come in to tell the "story so far" of the sessions to date. For each picture, remind them what it shows or invite them to articulate what it shows. For example:

God created the world.

God created Adam and then Eve.

Adam and Eve disobeyed God.

God sent them away from himself and his place because of their sin.

But God was still committed to being with his people, so he came to live with them in a tent.

But they were still separated from him. There was a "Keep Out" curtain.

God gave them a swap. One goat died to pay the penalty for their sin, and another goat took their sin away so that the could have God living among them.

Eventually a temple was built for God to live in with them. But the "Keep Out" curtain was still there. The people were still separated from God.

We're about to fast-forward through a LOT of history. A long time after that temple was built, it got to the stage where Israel had disobeyed God so much and so often and so completely that God sent them away from the temple. And what's more, God himself left the temple. But he also made a promise: that one day he would make a way for people to be with him again. "I will gather you … I will bring you home," he promised in Zephaniah 3 v 20.

And we're going to rejoin the story at the exciting moment that God kept his promise…

Let's Continue the Bible's Story

> *As you summarise the Bible's teaching on who Jesus is with reference to his divinity and his sinless humanity, here are some very basic suggestions for ways to engage the children visually or to give them opportunities to move about, and a script illustrating what this storytelling-and-explaining segment might sound like.*
>
> - *Have props and/or pictures for the different elements you'll touch on. If you use the script below you could use a baby doll, a baby's crib with "God with us" on the side to put the baby in, a small tent to then put the crib in, a clean white t-shirt to represent a sinless life, and props that hint at some of the miracles Jesus did (bread and fish, bandages, a toy boat and so on).*
>
> - *Rather than bringing out these props at the appropriate time, you could station them around the room as if walking through Jesus' life story, moving as a group while you teach. If you can have a cross elsewhere in the room to illustrate that that is what Jesus' life is moving towards, that could be where you sit later in the session as you discuss Jesus' achievement at the cross.*

Our true story begins with… a baby. But not just any baby. Most babies nowadays get announced to the world through a text message or a photo shared online, or possibly a line in a newspaper that a few people might notice.

But this baby's arrival was announced by angels! And men called Luke and Matthew wrote chapters about his birth that have been read by millions of people all round the world. This was one special baby!

Matthew wrote that the baby's arrival had been promised long ago. One of God's messengers, Isaiah, had written that a young woman would one day have a baby and "'call him Immanuel' (which means 'God with us')" (Matthew 1 v 23, NIV).

God with us! This baby's birth meant that God was going to come and be among people again!

In fact, another Bible writer called John reminds us that God had always been committed to being with his people. When he wrote about this baby's arrival, John said that God "became a man and lived among us" (John 1 v 14, ICB). The word he used for "lived" is "tabernacled". Do you remember the tabernacle? It was the tent where God had lived among the people of Israel. And now God was coming to live among people again. But this time things were different. This time God himself had come as a man.

And who was that man…? Jesus! Jesus was God with us, God come near, God living among us people as one of us.

BUT Jesus was not the same as us.

Firstly, Jesus always obeyed and loved God the Father. He always did what was right and good. He "committed no sin," we're told in 1 Peter 2 v 22.

Secondly, Jesus showed that he was God the Son by doing things that only God can do. Do you know any of the things Jesus said or did that showed he was God? Let's share some ideas now…

> ⓘ *Kids will most likely mention miracles such as calming the storm, walking on water, physical healings, spiritual healings, raising the dead, feeding thousands and so on. They may also mention details such as the fact that he knew what others were thinking; that he said he was fulfilling Old Testament prophecies; that he used God's covenant name I AM of himself. They may refer to his baptism or the transfiguration and God the Father's declaration there, too.*
>
> *Be ready to ask questions or give hints to help the group if ideas aren't forthcoming initially.*

Imagine seeing and hearing all that! Imagine being Jesus' friends. Imagine how amazing it must have been to spend time with him. If you'd lived then, you could have seen God and spoken to God and just enjoyed being with God!

But that was then. And this is now. What does Jesus coming then have to do with all of us who live a long time after this all happened?

Well, Jesus said that he had come to open the way back to being with God in God's wonderful place. Do you remember that Adam and Eve and all humanity were shut out of God's presence and God's place? Now listen to these words from John 14 v 6. Jesus said, "I am the way and the truth and the life. No one comes to the Father except through me" (NIV).

Jesus hadn't just come to be present with twelve disciples and some crowds in one small region 2,000 years ago.

He had come to make a way for people to enjoy being back with God again—a once-for-all way, a permanent way, a final way.

What was Jesus' plan? We'll find out shortly!

For now…

🏁 Let's Play a Game

OPTION 1

> ⓘ *A familiar game that allows children to let off steam and illustrates being stuck, unable to release yourself and needing a rescuer. Play Stuck in the Mud / Freeze Tag by appointing someone (or a small number of children) to be catchers. When they tag an individual, that person has to freeze with legs apart or arms out and can only be freed by another runner crawling through their legs or ducking under an arm. Play for as long as you want or until everyone's stuck.*

OPTION 2

> ⓘ *An activity that can involve less physical contact and which illustrates the idea of relying on someone else to tell you the way.*
>
> *Play Minefield: Divide the group into pairs or teams up to five children, and for each team set up an obstacle course made of cones, upturned cups, socks (or whatever you have available!)—objects they must avoid touching. One person on each team is blindfolded, while another guides them (either physically or through speaking to them) through the minefield. If you want the game to last a little longer, anyone who hits a "mine" has to go back to the start to try again once the rest of their team have had their turn. Play at least until everyone has had a turn or until one team has successfully navigated all their members through, or until it's time to move on.*
>
> *After they have played:*

In that game, you had to rely on someone else to get you out when you were stuck / tell you the way through. You couldn't deal with the problem you faced—you needed someone else to rescue you / tell you the way.

We heard Jesus' words earlier, saying that he had come to be the way by which people could come back to God the Father. He was the one who would deal with the problem of sin. He clearly had a plan. And that plan was… that he would die on a cross. What a strange plan! Why would God's the Son plan to die?

👂 Let's Hear from God

> ⓘ *The passage used below is from the NIRV translation, which renders some of the complex vocabulary and sentence structures in a more straightforward way. If you prefer to use another translation, you may need to explain some of the more technical terms to the children.*

For Younger Children

Do you remember the goats? The goats swapped with the people of Israel. One goat died and one goat was sent away to deal with sin.

I'm going to read you some verses from the book of Romans that are all about Jesus dying on a cross. As I read, listen out for anything that reminds you of the goats:

"Everyone has sinned. No one measures up to God's glory. The free gift of God's grace makes us right with him. Christ Jesus paid the price to set us free. God gave Christ as a sacrifice to pay for

sins through the spilling of his blood. So God forgives the sins of those who have faith."
(Romans 3 v 23-25)

- What happened to Jesus that also happened to the first goat? *(He died/he was a sacrifice/his blood was spilled)*
- We know that the goat sacrifice was an important swap. Who was Jesus swapping with when he died? *("Us", v 25; answers may also be "people", "everyone", "those who have faith". The next session looks at receiving salvation through repentant faith, which is why it is not majored on here.)*
- What happened to sins when Jesus died? *(They were paid for/they were forgiven)**

> ⓘ *Print out the cross picture provided for this session, with the cross shape cut out. Have a pen and sticky notes to hand.*

Look at this picture with me. What do you think all the pictures are showing?

> ⓘ *Children may just say what they think is going on in each picture. Some might suggest that the pictures show that those attitudes and behaviours were being punished at the cross.*

Let's think of other examples of ways in which we know we all sin with our words or our actions or our attitudes.

> ⓘ *Be ready to start off with a few examples of your own. As the children offer other ideas, write them on sticky notes and stick them onto the cross picture.*

Jesus' friend Peter said this: that Jesus "suffered once for sins. The one who did what is right suffered for those who don't do right. He suffered to bring you to God" (1 Peter 3 v 18, NIRV). As you say this, turn over the cross to show a clear, sinless blank cross on the other side.

Jesus paid the price for sin. Jesus removed sin.

For Older Children

> ⓘ *Do as above. If time allows and if appropriate for your particular group, at the point marked * you could include the following:*

Now let's think about what makes Jesus' swap different to the goat swap. Listen to what the writer of the letter to the Hebrews in the New Testament said when he compared the two swaps. As I read, listen out for what was different about Jesus' sacrifice…

"The same sacrifices have to be offered over and over again. They must be offered year after year." (Hebrews 10 v 1, NIRV)

"Those offerings remind people of their sins every year. It isn't possible for the blood of bulls and goats to take away sins." (v 3-4)

"We have been made holy because Jesus Christ offered his body once and for all time." (v 10)

"By that one sacrifice [Jesus] has made perfect forever those who are being made holy." (v 14)

- What made Jesus' swap different to the goat swap?
- Why is that very good news?

📖 Let's Continue the Bible's Story

On the cross, Jesus took our sin. All the bad things we do and all the sad things they cause—Jesus took them all from us. And when he did, something amazing, astonishing, astounding happened…

> ⓘ *Tell this part of the Bible story in a way that is as visually impactful and dramatic as possible. The curtain tearing is a BIG DEAL! Think about how you can enlist helpers and use your space, lighting, sound effects and props to help the children appreciate the climactic drama of the moment. If you have set up a large "Keep Out" curtain of your own, now is the time to tear it or pull it apart!*

"It was nine in the morning when they crucified him. The written notice of the charge against him read: THE KING OF THE JEWS.

"They crucified two rebels with him, one on his right and one on his left. Those who passed by hurled insults at him … In the same way the chief priests and the teachers of the law mocked him among themselves … Those crucified with him also heaped insults on him.

"At noon, darkness came over the whole land until three in the afternoon. And at three in the afternoon Jesus cried out in a loud voice, 'Eloi, Eloi, lema sabachthani?' (which means 'My God, my God, why have you forsaken me?') …

"With a loud cry, Jesus breathed his last.

> [Pause!]

"THE CURTAIN OF THE TEMPLE WAS TORN IN TWO FROM TOP TO BOTTOM!"

(Mark 15 v 25-27, 29, 31, 32b, 33-34, 37-38, NIV)

Jesus suffered, he was insulted and he died to pay the price for sin. Jesus suffered, he was insulted and he died to remove sin. By dealing with sin once and for all, Jesus made a way for people to be with God again. Jesus is the way to be with God. God had ripped up the "Keep Out" sign!

💬 What Does This Mean for Us?

At the beginning of our session, we were thinking about events that changed human history.

For Younger Children and children less familiar with the gospel

> ⓘ *Ask children to think individually about each of the following questions, then swap answers with a partner, and then share their ideas with the group.*

When Jesus died on the cross, it changed everything! From what we've seen today, how would you finish these sentences?

- Jesus' death on the cross was important because he died so that…
- When Jesus died on the cross, the curtain tore because…

Jesus died on the cross to take our sin, so all his friends can now go in!

For Older Children and children more familiar with the gospel

ⓘ *Ask children to think individually about each of the following questions, then swap answers with a partner, and then share their ideas with the group. Choose whichever questions you think will work best with your group.*

- How did Jesus' death change everything for humanity? OR Why is Jesus' death a crucial moment in human history?
- If a friend asked you why the crucifixion of Jesus is so important, what would you say?
- If a friend said Jesus' death was a failure, what would you say?
- What did Jesus' death achieve? Why is Jesus' death good news?
- Could you explain to someone how Jesus' death fits into the big story of the Bible?
- When you think about Jesus' death, what difference does it make to you?

Let's Talk to God about That

ⓘ *Here are a number of possible ways of encouraging the children to turn what they have learnt about Jesus and his substitutionary death into prayers of praise. You will need to judge what is appropriate for your group. They move loosely from most supported and least independent to most open and least scaffolded.*

1. Say sentences of praise such as the ones below and invite the children to say "WOW!" after each line:

   - *Jesus, you are God himself!*
   - *Jesus, you came to live as a human even though you made everything!*
   - *Jesus, you lived as a human, but you never did anything wrong!*
   - *Jesus, you had a plan to deal once and for all with the problem of sin!*
   - *Jesus, you suffered, you were insulted and you died to pay the penalty for sin!*
   - *Jesus, you are the way people can enjoying being back with God again!*
   - *Jesus, your death meant that God tore up the "Keep Out" sign!*

2. Discuss how they might finish these prayer sentence-starters and invite them to use them to pray or use their ideas to pray on their behalf:

   - *Perfect Lord Jesus, we praise you because you…*
   - *Loving Lord Jesus, we thank you for being willing to…*
   - *Wonderful Lord Jesus, we thank you that…*

3. Invite the children to take a moment to look quietly at your torn curtain (or a picture of the torn curtain). What did it take to open the way back to God? And what is now possible? How do those things make them feel? Begin a time of prayer in which they can pray aloud or in their head to tell God how they feel about that.

4. Ask the children what has most struck them:

> - *about who Jesus is.*
> - *what Jesus achieved.*
> - *about God's commitment to people.*
>
> *Is there anything that has been new for them or has puzzled or amazed them? What does it make them want to say to or ask God now? Give them the opportunity to pray individually either in their head or aloud.*

Let's Get Creative

Minimal resources:

You'll need paper and coloured pens or pencils. Give each child a part of the whole Bible story so far (or let them choose one), and ask them to draw that scene. Then invite the children to look at each other's pictures and identify which part of the Bible the picture is about.

Resources you may have available:

- You'll need the activity book accompanying *The Garden, the Curtain and the Cross*: cross drawing/writing page.
- You'll need scratch art crosses. Children can draw Jesus on one, or write their own name on it, or label it with examples of sins. Or they could write a summary message of the lesson on it: for instance, "He died on the cross to take our sin so all his friends can now go in".
- You'll need pre-purchased or homemade cross crafts. An online search brings up various possibilities: cross sun-catchers to colour in; wooden crosses to decorate with appropriate pens or stickers; lollypop/popsicle stick crosses to decorate; foam cross craft kits; fuzzy art crosses to colour in; making a cross out of beads.

More of a project:

- A cross collage: Provide magazines with pictures of people, and paper on which to write sinful behaviours and attitudes, and invite the children to design their own cross-shaped collage to illustrate what Jesus took at the cross.
- Whole-series project (see this section in Session 1 for more detail on this): Work together to make a larger version of the collage craft suggested above.

In the Week

If you'd like to suggest ways that families could enjoy continuing to think about the lesson in the week:

- For younger children: They could read *The Garden, the Curtain and the Cross* storybook together. Perhaps they could have take-home questions along the lines of "What happened when Jesus died on the cross?" and/or "What did the temple curtain tearing show Jesus had done?"
- Suggest families play Stuck in the Mud / Freeze Tag and talk about how Jesus is the one who came to save us because we can't save ourselves.

- Encourage children to learn a memory verse with their family or carer that celebrates what Christ achieved at the cross:

    "Christ died for sins once for all, the righteous for the unrighteous,
    to bring you to God."
    (1 Peter 3 v 18, NIV 1984)

SESSION 5
The Choice We All Face – Prepare Your Heart

📖 Read 1 Corinthians 15 v 1-11

- What reasons does Paul give us to be confident that Jesus really rose?
- How do verses 1-2 underline the importance of believing, and continuing to believe, the New Testament gospel?

When Paul wrote to the church in Corinth, he knew they were listening to some influential voices who were suggesting that physical resurrection from the dead was ridiculous. "I want to remind you," he said, "of the gospel I preached to you, which you received and on which you have taken your stand. By this gospel you are saved, if you hold firmly to the word I preached to you" (1 Corinthians 15 v 1-2). And here was his message: "that Christ died for our sins according to the Scriptures, that he was buried, that he was raise don the third day according to the Scriptures" (v 3-4). The resurrection of Jesus was and is central to the gospel. It stands as the historical proof that all that God promised in Scripture has been fulfilled; that all that Jesus claimed about his identity and mission was true; and that resurrection from the dead is not an impossibility but in fact is the future destiny for everyone who trusts in Jesus as their risen King.

Paul pointed to two reasons why we can have confidence that Jesus really rose. First, the resurrection took place "according to the Scriptures". God had promised he would do it centuries before; Jesus himself spoke of the "sign of Jonah", who was in the place of the dead, the belly of a fish, for three days and nights and yet rose from the depths of the seas to preach repentance (Matthew 12 v 40). Second, Jesus "appeared"—after his death, he was seen alive by hundreds of people on multiple occasions (1 Corinthians 15 v 4-6). *This really happened,* Paul is saying. *Yes, it was extraordinary, but it is also history.*

So the resurrection stands as the grounds of our confidence and as an invitation. It is the place we can take our doubts to when we wonder if we have taken our stand on sinking sand. And because Jesus has risen, proving himself to be the divine and rightful King of all people in all places at all times, we are invited to come in—to enter his kingdom, enjoying life with him as our King and looking forward to living in his presence eternally. All people must choose either to welcome this King or to resist him—to choose life with him or to face death without him. No one comes into God's presence automatically or by accident but only by declaring with their mouths and believing in their heart that Jesus is Lord, risen from the dead (Romans 10 v 9). So we hold out the gospel of the death and resurrection of Jesus to others, knowing that there is no one who cannot be saved and no one who does not need to be saved; and we continue to trust in the gospel ourselves. We have taken our stand, and staked our future, on the risen Jesus and his death for us.

Before you prepare to teach your group, and to ask them to consider their own response to the gospel, prepare your own heart. If you find yourself doubting or uncertain, take those doubts to the empty tomb. If you find yourself feeling low, let your feelings be shaped by the knowledge that you have a loving King who lives for ever and who has conquered death for you. If your witness to others is waning, challenge yourself with the risen Lord's call to "go and make disciples of all nations", calling them to enjoy his love and live for him for ever (Matthew 28 v 20)—starting with the children in your group.

- How are you ensuring you "hold firmly to the word" of the gospel message?
- How can you extend the gospel as an invitation to others this week?

SESSION 5
The Choice We All Face

3-5 year-olds

God's Word Tells Us...
Jesus rose from the dead to live and rule as King for ever. Jesus invites us to be his friends and live with him for ever.

1. Pray
Let's talk to God before we read the story:

Dear God, please teach us what happened to Jesus after he died and why it is good news. Amen.

2. Listen
Read *The Garden, the Curtain and the Cross* storybook from this page spread…

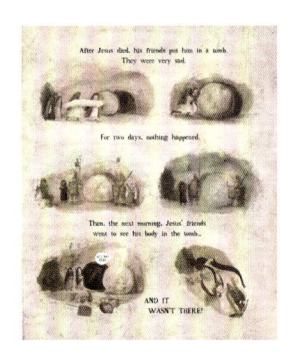

… up to and including the page spread that looks like this:

Some of the detail of the resurrection story is shown in the pictures rather than through the text here, so it's worth lingering on the images with the children. Here are a few ideas for how to make the reading interactive:

- Invite the children to act out the feelings of the characters at the different stages of the story on the resurrection pages—sadness, surprise or shock, excitement and happiness. Be ready to show them what those might look like.

- Draw attention to the REALLY BIG STONE in the first set of pictures and to the guards in the second set of pictures. No one was getting into that tomb!

- Invite the children to sit quietly for 10/20/30 seconds. It'll be hard! Imagine how the disciples felt waiting two whole days while nothing happened!

- Point to the angel telling them that Jesus wasn't there because he had risen. Why do the women look so excited, do they think?

- Before you read the second of the two page spreads, ask the children if they've ever received an invitation to a party or a wedding before.

3. Thinking
- Did Jesus stay dead?
- Did Jesus come back to life to invite his friends to live with God for ever?

- Does Jesus give people that same invitation today?

4. Game
Play "What's Missing" (a very simple version of the game often known as "Kim's Game"). Set up various trays with a small number of miscellaneous items on each. On each one, make sure there is some sort of man figure—a doll, a Lego figure, a photo of a person, a Playmobil figure. The children have a short amount of time to look at the handful of objects on the first tray and try to remember all of them. Re-cover the first tray and remove the man figure before showing the tray to the children again. Can they spot what's missing? Replay with the other trays, removing the human figure each time.

Then say:

"In that game, the man was gone each time. Jesus was gone from the tomb because he wasn't dead anymore. He was alive!"

OR

Play some sort of rolling game using balls or hoops. The children can aim for a target or try to get their ball or hoop the furthest or over a line.

Then say:

"In that game, you rolled the balls/hoops just like God rolled the stone away because Jesus wasn't dead anymore. He was alive!"

5. Summary Statement
Jesus rose from the dead to live and rule as King for ever. Jesus invites us to be his friends and live with him for ever.

6. Listen to God from the Bible
We know this because in Romans 10 verse 9 God says, "If you declare with your mouth, 'Jesus is Lord,' and if you believe in your heart that God raised Jesus from death, then you will be saved." (ICB)

7. Pray
Let's talk to God again now:

Lord Jesus, you rose from the dead to invite people to live with you for ever. Wow! Thank you, Jesus. You're amazing. Amen.

8. Craft Ideas
- Using card and/or paper plates, and split pins, children can colour and decorate an empty tomb. There are lots of designs online for simple empty tomb crafts where a stone "rolls" away, hinged on a split pin, to reveal an empty tomb (or the words "He is risen"). These could be pre-made for the children, who could then add colours, stickers, paper flowers and so on.
- Cover a plain, flat biscuit (UK) / cookie (US) with green icing to be the ground. Take another biscuit / cookie—ideally a ring-shaped one or a jammy dodger—and cut off part of it to create a semi-circular shape to be the "tomb". Stick it onto the other biscuit/cookie, by its flat edge, so that it is standing up. Then use a chocolate egg or button as the stone at the side of the cave entrance. (An internet search will bring up examples!)

SESSION 5
The Choice We All Face

5-12 year-olds

God's Word Tells Us...
Jesus rose from the dead! This means he has dealt with the problem of sin and death, and can offer his friends life for ever with him.

So What?
Jesus' resurrection means everyone faces a choice of whether to accept that offer. Let's think hard about our own response.

SECTION	PURPOSE	SUGGESTED ACTIVITY
Let's Get Ready Recap	Recap Sessions 1-4.	Short summary sentences for children to complete in a quick discussion.
Introduction	Introduce the idea of invitations.	An activity in which children have to match the party venue and party host.
Opening prayer	Pray for the session.	
Let's Continue the Bible's Story Bible teaching	Teach that Jesus rose from the dead to defeat sin and death, rule for ever, and invite people to eternal life.	Tell and explain the significance of the resurrection story in a way that: • emphasises that Jesus really rose and that eyewitnesses were sure of it. • emphasises that Jesus' death and resurrection fulfilled promises that God had made. • encourages children to consider how exciting it must have been. • establishes that Jesus' resurrection and ascension aren't the end of the story for Jesus' friends. (This is in preparation for next week's session.)

			A scripted example of what this might involve is given below and can be adapted to suit your age group and/or timings and/or personal storytelling style. There are also suggestions for how to make the storytelling visually engaging or to involve movement.
	Let's Play a Game	Provide a break for concentration. Emphasise the idea of celebration.	Different party games appropriate to your age range and setting.
	Let's Hear from God Bible teaching and discussion	Establish that the truths of Jesus' identity, death and resurrection require a response. Encourage the children to recognise and articulate the choice we all face: between repenting and trusting in Jesus or not. Show the result of repentance and belief: it brings the forgiveness of sin (and therefore enables God's presence with us—which will be dealt with more fully in the next session).	Age-appropriate Bible study and discussion questions from Acts 2. Can be done in smaller groups.
	So What Does this Mean for Us? Application	Give the children an opportunity to consider their own individual response.	A range of options that give all children to chance to engage with what they have heard in a way that is appropriate to them.
	Let's Talk to God about That Prayer	Give an example of appropriate response in prayer.	A teacher-led prayer that children can say "Amen" to or not, as they choose.
	Let's Get Creative Reinforcement	Enjoy an activity together that picks up on an element of the story, perhaps giving time for conversation with the children about what they think about what they've learned.	Craft activities: Various options requiring different levels of resourcing.
	At Home	Provide ways for families to continue thinking together about the invitation Jesus makes.	Various possible activities that pick up on or reinforce this session.

Let's Get Ready

… and do a super-quick summary of everything we've seen so far. I'll say the beginning of a sentence and you have to race to put your hand up with a suggestion to finish it off. Ready?

> ⓘ *Pick the first hand up (possibly leaving them out of the next "round" if there's a chance it'll be the same child each time!), but you could invite other ideas if there's time or if it would be helpful.*

- God made everyone to enjoy living…
- But everyone sins. Because of our sin we can't…
- God didn't turn his back on people even after…
- God promised to deal with the problem of…
- God the Son, Jesus, came to be the way…
- Jesus died…

Let's Start

… by thinking about party invitations. Who would be hosting the party if you received an invitation to:

- Buckingham Palace? *(The Queen/the Royal Family)*
- the White House/10 Downing Street? *(The President of the USA / the British Prime Minister)*
- the Emerald City? *(The Wizard of Oz)*
- The Isle of Berk? *(Stoick the Vast/Hiccup/their clan from the How to Train Your Dragon book series)*
- The Palace at Arendelle *(Elsa/Anna, from Frozen)*

If necessary, switch these examples for venues and hosts your children are likely to recognise. If each host is someone with power and authority, that relates well to the idea of receiving an invitation from God himself, but it's not essential.

Today we're going to be thinking about the most important invitation we'll ever receive. We'll think about who is making the invitation, what they're inviting people to, and how people respond to the invitation.

If you think about what we saw last time, it might seem strange to be thinking about celebrations and invitations. We left God's big Bible story at the point where Jesus died. That doesn't sound much like a party sort of moment, does it?

Let's Pray

Lord God, please excite us today with good news that is a reason to celebrate. Please show us the invitation you give us all and please show us how to respond. Amen.

📖 Let's Continue the Bible's Story

> ⓘ *As you tell the story of the resurrection and explain its significance, here are some very basic suggestions for ways to engage the children visually or give them opportunities to move about, plus a script illustrating what this storytelling-and-explaining segment might sound like.*
>
> - *Use the pictures provided for this session from the resurrection page spread in The Garden, the Curtain and the Cross to point to as you describe those events in your talk.*
> - *Invite the children to act out how they think Jesus' friends were feeling at different moments in the story. They can have fun really going wild with celebration at the appropriate point!*
> - *If you can devise a tomb model with a secret gap or door in the back, have someone place (for example) a Lego figure in it and then surreptitiously remove it via the back so that you can enact the big "JESUS WAS GONE!" moment.*

Imagine that you were one of Jesus' friends watching what happened to Jesus on the cross. Imagine that you were remembering all the time you had spent with Jesus before he died.

You'd think about all the things you had seen Jesus do—astonishing things, astounding things, things that only the amazing God himself could do. You'd remember all the times that you had walked with God and talked with God and enjoyed being with God.

And maybe you'd think of the times when Jesus had warned you that one day he wouldn't be with you anymore. You might remember that he'd explained "that he must be killed and on the third day be raised to life" (Matthew 16 v 21, NIV). But you hadn't really understood, and you certainly hadn't expected Jesus to end up on a cross.

Now Jesus is dead! Jesus is gone! What terrible sadness. What terrible disappointment. What terrible loss.

Let's listen to the Bible story now to find out what happened to Jesus and to those friends after the cross…

For two days of sadness, nothing happened.

Then, early on the Sunday morning, some of the women who had seen where Jesus' body had been placed went to the tomb where it was lying. They went to put special spices on his body.

But what was waiting for them was not what they expected. The stone covering the tomb was GONE! The body was GONE! Where had Jesus GONE?

Luke 24 verse 4 tells us that "While they were wondering about this, suddenly two men in clothes that gleamed like lightning stood beside them" (NIV).

- Who do you think they were? *(angels)*

Verses 5-6 continue, "The men said to them, 'Why do you look for the living among the dead? He is not here; he has risen!'" (NIV).

- What do you think they meant by "risen"? *(come back to life)*

Well, the women told the disciples, and some of those disciples rushed to see for themselves, and they found it just as the women said. Stone GONE! Body GONE! Where had Jesus GONE?

Later that day, Jesus' friends were all together, talking about what had happened.

And suddenly… Jesus. Was. THERE! Jesus ALIVE! Jesus AMONG THEM! Jesus COME BACK!

And Jesus said to them, *Look! Feel!* "Touch me and see," Jesus said in Luke 24 v 39 (NIV). And they saw him eat, and they felt his body. Jesus was real. Jesus was alive again.

And Jesus said to them, *Listen! Understand!* Verse 45 says that "he opened their minds so they could understand the Scriptures" (NIV). He explained to them how all of the promises God had made in the Old Testament had been leading to this moment:

God had said he would come and live among people. And he had come as Jesus, God the Son.

God had said that he would make a way for his people to live with him again. And Jesus had come and said, "I am the way".

God had said he would deal with the problem of sin once and for all. And Jesus had died for sin to rescue people from punishment for sin.

God had said the mighty rescuer would rise again to rule for ever. And that is just what Jesus had done.

Imagine his friends' astonishment. Imagine their amazement. Imagine their joy and their excitement. Do you think they jumped and whooped? Or maybe just stood there with their mouths open and eyes wide? Do you think they sang? And danced? Or turned cartwheels?! What do you think you would have done?

Over the next 40 days, Jesus appeared to many, many people, and he spent time with his disciples. He was getting them ready for a day when he would go away again, when he would go back to heaven.

But this time he made another promise. Jesus, Immanuel, the name that means "God with us", said to them, in Matthew 28 v 20, "You can be sure that *I will be with you always*" (ICB, emphasis added).

You see, Jesus going back to heaven wouldn't be the final chapter of the big Bible story of God with his people. There is more to come—and we will find out all about that next week!

But for now, let's celebrate with the disciples that Jesus rose to beat death and sin; that Jesus rose to be King for ever; that Jesus rose to offer his friends life with him for ever.

🏁 Let's Play a Game

In fact, let's play *lots* of games as we have our own celebration!

> ⓘ *Play as many games as will work in the time you have that are appropriate for the age of the children and the space. If balloons can be involved in some way, all the better! Try to create a party atmosphere. The aim of these games is simply to capture the mood of celebration and excitement among the disciples and to reinforce the idea of a party in order to tee up the concept of invitation and response in the second Bible-teaching segment.*
>
> *Easy party games that are appropriate if you need to avoid physical contact might include musical statues or "Kim's Game". Otherwise you can enjoy, for example, musical chairs, balloon races (over-under, passing along a line without using hands), other types of races (such as egg and spoon races), balloon volleyball, or minute-to-win-it games…*
>
> *After you finish:*

I imagine many of us have enjoyed games like those before at parties. Now, the thing about celebrations like that is you don't just turn up! The person who is hosting gets to decide who comes in. You receive an invitation, and then you have to reply, saying, "Yes please" or "No thank you". Now we're going to think about what it looks like to reply to God's invitation.

👂 Let's Hear from God

… as we hear from Acts chapter 2 about what happened one day, after Jesus had gone back to heaven, when Jesus' disciple Peter told a huge crowd of people all about Jesus.

For Younger Children

As I read, you'll need to do some actions. I will read out the sentences from the Bible one or two at a time.

If that sentence is a truth Peter told them about Jesus, cup your ear as if you're listening to Peter.

If that sentence is a way that the people responded to what Peter said, cover your heart as if you're feeling what they felt.

If that sentence is an instruction Peter gave them, hold up a finger as if you're telling someone what they need to do.

If that sentence is a promise Peter gave them, give a thumbs up as if you're receiving good news.

> *Recap the actions as you say:*

Truth… response… instruction… or promise.

Let's practise with some other sentences:

- Jesus is God! [pause for action] That's a truth.
- We feel amazed! What shall we say? [pause for action] That's a response.
- You need to turn back to God! [pause for action] That's an instruction.
- God will put things right! [pause for action] That's a promise.

Ok, let's go! Here are some of the things Peter said when he was speaking to a crowd, from Acts 2 v 22-38 (NIRV):

"Fellow Israelites … Jesus of Nazareth was a man who had God's approval. God did miracles, wonders and signs among you through Jesus." *(Truth, about who Jesus is)*

"Long ago God planned that Jesus would be handed over to you … You nailed him to the cross. But God raised him from the dead." *(Truth, about Jesus' death and resurrection)*

"You nailed Jesus to the cross. But God has made him both Lord and Messiah [the promised, forever King]." *(Truth, about Jesus ruling for ever)*

"When the people heard this, it had a deep effect on them. They said to Peter and the other apostles, 'Brothers, what should we do?'" *(Response)*

"Peter replied, 'All of you must turn away from your sins and be baptized in the name of Jesus Christ'." *(Instructions)*

"Then your sins will be forgiven. You will receive the gift of the Holy Spirit." *(Promise)*

Great job on the actions! Next, how are you at playing True or False?!

I'm going to say some more sentences that put what we've just heard in my own words. But sometimes I might get it wrong. You have to tell me if what I say is true (nod/thumbs up) or false (shake/thumbs down):

- Peter told them Jesus is God's King, that he did amazing miracles, that he died and that he rose again. *(True)*

- The people who heard this carried on as normal. *(False—they saw that the truths about Jesus needed to make a difference and they asked what they should do.)*

- Peter told them to turn away from sin, which means turn back to God. *(True—the special word Peter used was "repent", which means turn round, turn back to God.)*

- Peter told them that now they trusted Jesus, they could show their trust by being baptised. *(True)*

- Peter said their sins would still be a problem. *(False—he said their sins would be forgiven.)*

- Peter told them that the Holy Spirit, God himself, would come and be with them. *(True—their sin had been forgiven for ever and now God could live with them for ever.)*

For Older Children

Read Acts 2 v 22-24, 32-33, 36-38

> *The questions have been written based on the NIRV version, though differences in translation are referenced below.*

- What truths about Jesus did the crowd hear from Peter (v 22-24, 32-33, 36)? *(Who he was, and is—God, the promised forever King; what he did—his miracles, his planned death, his resurrection.)*

- Read verse 37. How did they respond to hearing those truths? *(They were deeply affected; they wanted to know what they should do.)*

Peter gave them two instructions in reply:

- According to verse 38 they were to be baptised.* They were to go down into the water and come back up out again to show they were putting their trust in the one who went down to death for them and rose again to save them from sin. Who is that? *(Jesus Christ)*

- What else did verse 38 tell them to do? *(Turn away from your sins/repent/change your hearts and lives—depending on the translation you use.)*

- Have you come across the word "repent" before, which is translated here as "turn away from your sins/change your hearts and lives"? What do you understand "repent" to mean? *(Possible answers: turn round, turn back to God, turn away from sin, say sorry for sin, confess sin, live with God in charge, live God's way not my way.)*

- Look at verse 38. When people repent (turn back to God and turn away from sin) and trust in Jesus, what two things happen? *(Their sins are forgiven, and they receive the gift of the Holy Spirit.)*

We are going to think more about the Holy Spirit next week. Today we're going to focus instead on the idea of responding to the truths about Jesus that we've seen in this passage.

> ⓘ * *Your church will have its own theological view of who the Bible encourages to be baptised: those who are professing belief themselves and/or the children of believing parents. So, if children in your group ask about who should be baptised, you can answer that here in Acts 2, these are unbaptised people who have just put their faith in Jesus, and this is the right way to show that they have done so; and then explain your own church's position on questions about baptism.*

💬 What Does This Mean for Us?

Just like that crowd in the book of Acts, we have heard a lot of truths in recent weeks. We have heard that:

- God made people to enjoy living with him.

- All people choose to turn their back on God. Sin means we can't live with him.

- But God did not turn his back on people even after they turned their back on him. God had a plan to deal with sin once and for all.

- God the Son, Jesus, came to earth to live as a man. He never sinned. Jesus died on the cross to take the punishment people deserve for sin.

- He rose from the dead to defeat sin for ever, rule for ever and offer life for ever.

And we have heard another very important truth. God tells us that just as Adam and Eve faced a choice in Eden, just as that crowd in Jerusalem faced a choice, everyone today faces a choice:

- When we hear about Jesus the King, will we repent? Will we say, "I don't want to live turning my back on God. I want to turn back to him"?

- And when we hear about Jesus the Rescuer, will we trust in him? Will we believe that he died for our sin and rose so that we can enjoy life with him for ever?

Some of us may never have heard those truths before and might be thinking about our response for the first time.

Some of us may have heard those truths before and have questions we want to ask.

Some of us may have heard those truths about Jesus, and we already live repenting and trusting Jesus every day.

Some of us may have heard those truths before, and now we want to repent and trust in Jesus for the first time.

So we might each want to use the next few minutes a bit differently from each other. Here are some options for you to choose from. We're all going to take x minutes in quiet on our own to do the activity we choose. This time is just for you, so don't worry about what other people are doing.

> ⓘ *These are suggestions for positive options you can give the children, so that they don't necessarily have to share their response and don't feel coerced into making one. You know your children and what sort of response activities would be appropriate for them.*
>
> *For younger children, limit the number of options. You could just say your list of options to them, or you may want to represent them visually in some way to help them remember them and choose one. Have pieces of paper and pens to hand.*

- I want to draw/write about what I've learnt today.
- I want to draw/write about how I feel about what I've learnt today.
- I want to draw/write a question I have.*
- I want just to sit and think about it some more.
- I want to ask God to help me to understand/respond/trust.
- I do trust that Jesus is King and Rescuer—I want to say thank you to him for…
- I do trust in Jesus and I want to keep turning back to God whenever I sin, so I want to say sorry for something I know I shouldn't have done.
- I believe these truths and now I want to repent and put my trust in Jesus. I want to know what to say to God.**

> ⓘ ** Have a question box for these questions to be placed in anonymously. You could take questions out and answer them during any craft time (and if not, make sure that you do answer them, whether in this session or the next one).*
>
> *** Have a simple response prayer printed ready, based on the prayer in the next "Let's Talk to God about That" section. If one of the children asks for this, make sure you follow up with them and their parents or care-giver.*
>
> *Once the children have had time to respond in the way that each of them has chosen, lead them in a prayer such as the one below.*

🙏 Let's Talk to God about That

I am going to pray now. If you agree with my prayer and want it to be what you say to God too, you can say "Amen". Feel free to sit and listen and think quietly if you prefer.

Lord Jesus, we praise you because you are mighty God, the forever King, the sin-defeating Rescuer.

We thank you for being willing to die for sin. We thank you that you rose from the dead to offer your friends life with you for ever. We thank you that you forgive sins and give the gift of your Spirit.

Heavenly Father, we are sorry for the ways that we disobey you and treat others badly. Please forgive us.

Please keep reminding us of all the truths we have learnt. Please keep reminding us of the good news. Please show us when we sin. Please give us hearts that every day want to say sorry and turn away from sin. Please give us hearts that every day trust in Jesus' death and resurrection for our rescue. Amen.

Let's Get Creative

Minimal resources:

- You'll need paper and coloured pens or pencils. Children can choose to draw the scene at the empty tomb or when Jesus appeared to his disciples, or to draw emojis for all the different emotions Jesus' friends experienced from his death on the cross onwards, or to design an invitation from God to people to enjoy life for ever with him in his perfect place (encourage them to include details on how to "RSVP").

Resources you may have available:

- You'll need the activity book accompanying *The Garden, the Curtain and the Cross*: wordsearch number 2; the drawing faces page, either to be used as suggested or as templates for children to draw the different emotions Jesus' friends experienced in the Bible story.

- You'll need card or paper plates, and split pins. There are lots of designs online for simple empty-tomb crafts where a stone "rolls" away hinged on a split pin to reveal an empty tomb.

- You'll need: biscuits/cookies, green icing, chocolate eggs/chocolate buttons. Cover a plain, flat biscuit (UK) / cookie (US) with green icing to be the ground. Take another biscuit / cookie—ideally a ring-shaped one or a jammy dodger—and cut off part of it to create a semi-circular shape to be the "tomb". Stick it onto the other biscuit/cookie, by its flat edge, so that it is standing up. Then use a chocolate egg or button as the stone at the side of the cave entrance. (An internet search will bring up examples!)

- More of a project:

- Make an Easter tomb garden using a plastic tray, half a plastic cup for the tomb, a stone for the entrance, wooden crosses made from lolly/popsicle sticks or wooden skewers, soil to fill the tray and cover the surface of the cup, and fast-growing seeds such as cress. You can add other details such as paper towel grave clothes, and the children can take the whole thing home with instructions for watering!

- Whole series project (see this section in Session 1 for more detail on this): Children could help paint and add detail to an already-made papier-mâché tomb.

At Home

If you'd like to suggest ways that families could enjoy continuing to think about the lesson in the week:

- For younger children: They could read *The Garden, the Curtain and the Cross* storybook together. Perhaps they could have take-home questions along the lines of "What happened to Jesus after his dead body was put in the tomb?" and/or "What invitation does Jesus give to people?"

- Suggest families play their own easy party games and discuss what Jesus has invited his friends to and how we say "Yes please" to that invitation—we repent and believe in Jesus Christ.

- Encourage children to learn a memory verse with their family or carer that articulates the choice that Christ's resurrection leaves us with:

    > "If you declare with your mouth, 'Jesus is Lord,' and believe in your heart
    > that God raised him from the dead, you will be saved."
    > (Romans 10 v 9, NIV)

SESSION 6
Life and the Last Garden - Prepare Your Heart

Read Revelation 21 v 1-5; 22 v 1-6

- How would you describe the relationship between God and his people that we see in this glimpse of eternity to come?
- How does 21 v 3-4 comfort and excite you today?

This is a thrilling time to be alive, and there's an infinitely more thrilling time to come.

Our current age is the age between Jesus' first coming to bring grace to his people and his second coming in glory at the end of human history (Titus 2 v 11-14). And it is an exciting time to be a member of God's people because (and unlike in Old Testament times) God is present not near his people (in the tabernacle or the Jerusalem Temple) but *in* his people. At Pentecost, ten days after Jesus' ascension to his Father's side in heaven, the Spirit was poured out on all believers (Acts 2 v 1-1-21).

And so you have the great privilege of yourself being a temple of God, the place of his presence (1 Corinthians 6 v 19-20); or, to put it another way, of being a living stone in the temple of God's presence, his gathered believers—what we call the church (1 Peter 2 v 4-6; Ephesians 2 v 19-22). The Spirit's ministry in his people is fundamental to both the start and continuation of our Christian lives—he is crucial if we are to become more like Jesus and tell others about Jesus. Remembering this causes those of us who are by nature "can-do" people to stop and pray and rely on him, and those of us who are by nature "can't-do" people to take risks by relying on him.

Another aspect of the Spirit's ministry is to remind us that we are God's children and assure us that we will enjoy eternity in his presence (Romans 8 v 16-23). One day, Jesus will return, without warning (Matthew 24 v 44), and restore this world to its original "very-goodness": a world without sin, where justice has been done and God's perfected people live in resurrection bodies; and therefore where nothing bad and nothing sad ever happens. Every tear will be dried (Revelation 21 v 3-4), and the tree of life will once more be available (22 v 2). But there will be no tree of the knowledge of good and evil, because God's people will have already chosen his rule instead of theirs, and so, at the centre, will stand his throne (22 v 1). He will be fully, gloriously present with his people: "God's dwelling-place is now among the people, and he will dwell with them" (21 v 3). However great life is now, a Christian's best days lie ahead. And however hard life is now, a Christian can know that one day all hardship will lie in the past.

So, before you prepare to teach your group, prepare your own heart. In what areas does the knowledge of your perfect future in God's presence need to give you perspective? If we are investing too much in the things of this world (money, possessions, experiences, relationships), we can remember that the new creation holds far greater pleasures than this one. If we feel weary of the Christian life in the struggles and sufferings and disappointment, we can encourage our hearts today with the thought that Jesus is coming back. If we find ourselves shrink back from sharing our faith instead of taking risks to do so, we can trust the Spirit to work powerfully through us as we share the gospel. Truly, the knowledge of eternity changes everything. So we live today remembering that one day Jesus is going to make all things new; and we live today remembering that it might just be today that he does so!

- How could knowing the Spirit dwells in you shape your thoughts and plans today?
- Your best days will come after Jesus returns. How does that make you feel?

SESSION 6
Life and the Last Garden

3-5 year-olds

God's Word Tells Us…
One day Jesus' friends will live with him for ever in a perfect world, where there won't be anything bad or sad. We will enjoy being with God, and we will say, "Thank you Jesus!"

1. Pray
Let's talk to God before we read the story:

Dear God, please make us excited about the perfect world you invite people to. Amen.

2. Listen
Read *The Garden, the Curtain and the Cross* storybook from this page spread…

… up to and including the page spread that looks like this:

A page spread from last session's reading is deliberately repeated. Here are a few ideas for how to make the reading interactive:

- On this page, you could invite them to say what animals they can spot. You could ask them which person in the picture they think is Jesus—he's the King welcoming his friends to his perfect world.

- Can they spot any warrior angels in the picture? In this picture, are those warrior angels saying "Keep Out" or "Come In"?

- Before reading the last page, you could ask the children what they say to someone who gives them a gift or invites them to a party.

3. Thinking
- Will Jesus' friends enjoy being with God one day? Will they live in a perfect place with nothing bad and no one sad?
- Who do we say "Thank you" to for dying and rising to make that possible?

4. Game
Play party games to celebrate the good news that one day Jesus' friends will live with him for ever in a perfect world, where there won't be anything bad or sad. These might include:

- Duck Duck Goose
- Pin the tail
- Under and Over games (with, for instance, balloons)
- Egg and Spoon races
- Musical Statues / Freeze Dance
- a scavenger hunt
- Pass the Parcel (in which case, it would be good to have a prize in every layer and a final prize that can be shared among the group)

Then say:

"Our little party was full of laughing and playing and smiling and fun. Won't it be wonderful to live with God in a world that is full of happiness all the time?!"

[Or, if kids got angry/upset/whiny at any point during the games]

"We just had a lovely party. But even in our short party there were things that made us feel upset or grumpy. Jesus says that one day his friends will get to live with him, and there will never be anything to make us feel upset or grumpy. Wow!"

5. Summary Statement
One day Jesus' friends will live with him for ever in a perfect world, where there won't be anything bad or sad. We will enjoy being with God, and we will say, "Thank you Jesus!"

6. Listen to God from the Bible
We know this because in Revelation 21 verses 3-4 God tells us about what his perfect world will be like for his friends. The Bible says, "[God] will live with them, and they will be his people. God himself will be with them and will be their God. He will wipe away every tear from their eyes. There will be no more death, sadness, crying, or pain. All the old ways [will be] gone." (ICB)

7. Pray
Let's talk to God again now:

Lord God, you will make the world perfect again. And you will live with your people again. Wow! Thank you, Jesus. You're amazing. Amen.

8. Craft Ideas
- Use the "Living with God" page in the activity book for children to draw on/colour/paint/add stickers to. As they enjoy crafting or colouring, remind them that the best thing of all will be that God will be there.

- Make party paper chains. Children can draw smiley faces on pre-cut strips of paper and glue them to make paper chains (with help if necessary). As they enjoy crafting or colouring, remind them that in God's perfect world there will be nothing bad and no one sad, and that the best thing of all will be that God will be there.

- Pre-cut paper chain people for the children to decorate with smiling faces and colour in and/or stick white robes to. As they enjoy colouring or crafting, remind them that Jesus promises his friends that they will all live with him one day in a world where there will be nothing bad and no one sad.

SESSION 6
Life and the Last Garden

5-12 year-olds

God's Word Tells Us...
God lives with his people now by his Holy Spirit. One day God's people will live with him for ever in perfect relationship in a perfect world.

So What?
We have a LOT to praise God for now and a LOT to look forward to!

SECTION	PURPOSE	SUGGESTED ACTIVITY
Let's Get Ready Introduction	Introduce the idea of happy endings involving reunions.	Quick discussion activities matching film endings to characters.
Opening prayer	Pray for the session.	
Recap	Recap Sessions 1-5 to lead into the Bible storytelling segment next.	Children act out summaries of what they have learnt in previous weeks.
Let's Continue the Bible's Story Bible teaching	Tell the events of Pentecost as part of the story of God's ongoing commitment to being present with his people. Teach that God is present by His Spirit with all who repent and believe in Jesus. Establish that God is not only with his people by His Spirit, but He also works in and for them, by touching very briefly on some examples of the work of the Spirit in God's people today.	Share the story of Pentecost, the promise that God is with his people now by that same Spirit, and some of the ways that God's Spirit works in and for us. A scripted example of what this might involve is given below and can be adapted to suit your age group and/or timings and/or personal storytelling style. There are also suggestions for how to make the storytelling visually engaging or to involve movement.

🏁	**Let's Play a Game**	Provide a break for concentration.	
		Illustrate some of the work of the Holy Spirit in his people today.	"Blob"—a tag-style game in which the team grows as people are caught.
		OR	
		Illustrate the idea of bringing people back together.	A hunt for puzzle pieces to put back together.
👂	**Let's Hear from God** Bible teaching and discussion	Teach that Jesus will return to take his friends to live for ever with God in the new creation, highlighting that: • God will live for ever with his people without separation and in restored relationship. • life there will be eternal, sinless and unspoilt. • everything that was lost in Genesis 3 will be restored: presence, relationship, life.	Age-appropriate Bible study and discussion questions from Revelation 21 – 22. Can be done in smaller groups.
💬	**What Does This Mean for Us?** Application	Invite the children to reflect on what has most struck and/or excited them and help them consider how to turn that response into prayer.	Open-ended discussion questions for use as a whole class or in smaller groups. Suggested questions are given on page 96.
🙏	**Let's Talk to God about That** Prayer	Give opportunities to praise God for what you have seen about him in this session and in the whole series.	A number of different options depending on the circumstances of the group.
🎨	**Let's Get Creative** Reinforcement	Enjoy an activity together that picks up on an element of the story, perhaps giving time for conversation with the children about what they think about what they've learned.	Craft activities: Various options requiring different levels of resourcing.
🏠	**At Home**	Provide ways for families to continue thinking together about God's presence now by his Spirit and his forever, perfect presence in the new creation.	Various possible activities that pick up on or reinforce this session.

Let's Get Ready

ⓘ *If you think it would help, find pictures of the relevant characters to show the children as you do this activity.*

I'm going to ask you questions about some famous films. Let's see who can race to put their hands up with the answer:

- Which two characters end up reunited with Andy in Andy's car at the end of *Toy Story*? *(Woody and Buzz)*
- Which character ends up reunited with Nala and his family at Pride Rock at the end of *The Lion King*? *(Simba)*
- Which character ends up reunited with her sister and the people of Arendelle at the end of *Frozen*? *(Elsa)*

ⓘ *Add other examples if you wish; they need to involve people being reunited and returning to a place.*

Happy endings in books and films often involve people overcoming problems, returning to a special place and being reunited with someone the character loves.

So with the help of Buzz and other friends, in *Toy Story* Woody is rescued from distance and difficulty and his dastardly enemy, Sid, to be reunited with his owner, Andy. In *The Lion King*, with the help of Pumbaa and Timon and the pride, Simba is rescued from self-hate and self-doubt to overcome his sinister enemy, Scar, and be reunited with his mother and his beloved Nala. With the help of Anna *[pronounced "Arna"!]*, in *Frozen* Elsa is rescued from fear and frozen powers and her fierce enemy, Hans, to be reunited safely with her people and her family.

At the end of the films, Woody, Simba and Elsa are all excited about being home—but they didn't long for home because of their comfy bed, or the meal that awaited them, or because they were looking forward to a hot bath. They longed for that place because they longed for the person who was waiting for them there.

I love it when films end like this! I bet you do too. I think the reason we love these kinds of endings is because in a way all these stories are mini versions of a much bigger story—the Bible's story. Today we're going to be thinking about where we are today in the Bible's big story and where that story is heading for its very happy ending.

Let's Pray

Lord God, please excite us about the happy ending you have planned for your friends, and show us how you are with your people today as they wait for that happy ending. Amen.

Let's Look Back

As we get ready to hear from the Bible, let's remind ourselves what we've seen so far.

I'll read out a summary of what we've seen so far, and I'll pause for you to act out what I've said. Let's see who's got good ideas:

- In the first garden, God lived with Adam and Eve. They could walk with him and talk with him and just enjoy being with him.

- But Adam and Eve, and every person since, turned their back on God. So he says, *Because of your sin, you can't come in.*

- The amazing thing is, even after people turned their back on God, God didn't turn his back on them; he made a way to live among them. He told them to build a tent… and then a temple.

- So that sinful people could have the sinless God live among them, God made a swap to pay for people's sin. One goat died… and the other goat was sent away.

- But sin was still a problem, and so there was a big curtain that was God's way of saying "Keep Out".

- So God made a once-for-all solution to the problem of sin. God the Son came and lived among people as a man—Jesus.

- Jesus died on the cross to take the punishment we deserve for sin.

- When Jesus died, the curtain tore from top to bottom to show that Jesus had made a way back for us to be with God.

- Jesus rose from the dead to give his friends life with him for ever.

Well done! Big round of applause! Let's sit down again…

After Jesus had risen from the dead, Jesus returned to heaven. He is there now, waiting for the day he will come back to take his friends to be with him. So if he is there and we are here, how is God living with his people today?

📖 Let's Continue the Bible's Story

> ⓘ *As you tell the story of Pentecost and explain its significance, here are some very basic suggestions for ways to engage the children visually/aurally or give them opportunities to move about, plus a script illustrating what this storytelling-and-explaining segment might sound like.*
>
> - *Have two different spaces for "inside" (where Jesus' followers receive the Spirit) and "outside" (where they tell the crowds about Jesus), and move between the two spaces at that point in the story to give a quick break for movement.*
>
> - *Invite the children to make the sounds of the wind and to flutter their hands to represent flame at that point in the story. You could ask them to close their eyes at that point and try to imagine what the early disciples heard and saw.*
>
> - *Invite the children to speak in other languages they may know at that point in the story.*

We find the answer to the question of how God is living with his people today in the book of Acts, which tells us the history of the early church. Before he went to heaven, Jesus told his friends in Acts 1 v 4, "Do not leave Jerusalem … Wait for the gift my Father promised" (NIRV). And who had God the Father promised to send? Verse 8 tells us—Jesus promised that "the Holy Spirit will come to you" (ICB)—that's God the Spirit, God himself.

Jesus thought this was such exciting news that he even said to his disciples, in John 16 v 7, "It is better for you that I go away. When I go away I will send the Helper [the Holy Spirit] to you" (ICB). What could be better than walking and talking and enjoying being with Jesus?! Well, Jesus said that having the Holy Spirit come to live with them would be. How exciting is that?!

So, what happened? Listen to these events that Luke wrote about in Acts 2 v 2-3:

Not long afterwards, Jesus' friends were all together in one place. "Suddenly a sound like the blowing of a violent wind came from heaven and filled the whole house where they were sitting" (NIV). Then "they saw something that looked like fire in the shape of tongues. The flames separated and came to rest on each of them. All of them were filled with the Holy Spirit" (NIRV).

On that day, God showed them by sounds and sights outside of them what God was doing inside of them. God was breathing his Holy Spirit into them, so they heard a strong wind. God himself, symbolised by fire, was coming to live in them, so they saw flames. That very first time, God gave them the sound of the wind and the sight of the fire to show them that this was God at work, keeping his promise.

And so that other people could also know that God had just done something amazing, God did something that only God can do: the Holy Spirit gave Jesus' friends the ability to "speak in languages they had not known before", as it says in verse 4 (NIRV), so that they could tell all the visitors to Jerusalem about Jesus. Something very exciting had just happened as God kept his promise to come and live with Jesus' friends.

And the excitement is for us too! After he received the Holy Spirit, Peter straight away told the crowds about Jesus—we heard some of what he said last time. The crowds heard the truths about Jesus and wanted to know how to respond. So Peter said to them in verses 38-39, "Turn away from your sins and be baptized in the name of Jesus Christ. Then your sins will be forgiven. You will receive the gift of the Holy Spirit. The promise is for you and your children. It is also for all who are far away. It is for all whom the Lord our God will choose" (NIRV).

Peter was explaining that God comes to live with ALL his friends in ALL times and ALL places by his Holy Spirit. In Matthew 28 v 20 Jesus says to all his friends, "You can be sure that I am always with you" (NIRV), and he is with us by his Spirit.

And do you know what? The excitement doesn't stop there! Because the Holy Spirit isn't just God with us. He is God for us. He is here to help us. And if I tried to share all the ways the Holy Spirit works in us and for us and through us, we'd be here all day! So I'm going to tell you as many as I can in 45 seconds! There's X seconds on the clock. Are you ready?!

> ⓘ *Before the session, time yourself saying the list below at speed and then set your clock accordingly so that you don't finish before the clock does (and if you do, give yourself less than 45 seconds). The point is not to send the children away knowing an exhaustive list of the works of the Spirit (this isn't one!) but rather to send them away with the impression that God's Spirit is active in and for us in our lives.*

The Holy Spirit is at work when God saves someone from sin and gives them new life (Titus 3 v 5); he helps people share the good news about Jesus (1 Peter 1 v 12) and makes their message powerful (1 Thessalonians 1 v 5); he gives Jesus' friends special gifts and abilities to enable them to serve one another; he teaches us to need one another (1 Corinthians 12); he grows in us actions and attitudes that God loves, and we call these the fruit of the Spirit (Galatians 5 v 22-23); the Holy Spirit gives us power to say "no" to sin (Romans 8 v 13); he tells us that we're God's children (Romans 8 v 16); the Holy Spirit prays for us and helps us when we don't know what to pray (Romans 8 v 26); he gives us wisdom and understanding so that we can know God better (Ephesians 1 v 17) and so that we can understand what God has done for us in Jesus (1 Corinthians 2 v 12); the Holy Spirit gives Jesus' friends delight in sharing life with one another (2 Corinthians 13 v 14); he is there with us even when other people treat us badly because we believe in Jesus Christ (1 Peter 4 v 14)…

See, I told you there was lots to get excited about!

And do you know what? The excitement doesn't stop there, either! Even after the garden and the cherubim and the flaming sword and the tabernacle and the temple and the curtain and God himself on earth in Jesus and the cross and the resurrection and the coming of the Holy Spirit and everything the Holy Spirit does as he lives with Jesus' friends today [big breath!], we've STILL not reached the most exciting chapter of the story of how God lives with his people. We've got one more true story to go. We're going back to a garden.

But first…

🏁 Let's Play a Game

OPTION 1

> ⓘ *A game that gives an opportunity to run around and let off steam, and which (loosely!) illustrates some of the work of the Holy Spirit in calling people to "Team Jesus", uniting them to one another and equipping them to serve one another and make new disciples.*
>
> *Mark out a space that the children must stay inside. Depending on how large a group you have, assign one or more children to be catchers. Their task is to tag other children, at which point the tagged child joins the group by holding hands. Every time someone is tagged, they are added to the chain of children holding hands. They have to move together to enable the two children at either end who have free hands to continue tagging other players until everyone has been welcomed into the group. If numbers are large, you could have more than one chasing group to illustrate different bodies (churches) working in different places for the same purpose.*

In that game the line of people was like Jesus' church: it grew and grew, and everyone worked together to gather more people. That is one of the ways in which the Holy Spirit works in Jesus' friends, and one of the things all the people on Jesus' "team" have in common is that they all have God with them.

OPTION 2

> ⓘ *A game that reinforces the idea of bringing people back together.*
>
> *Put your children into groups of three or four. For each group, print a picture of a couple, a family or some film characters being reunited. Cut each picture up, making the number of pieces and complexity of shapes appropriate to the age of the children. For each group choose a number or symbol and write that on the back of each puzzle piece belonging to that group, and then hide them all around the room. The children have to find all the puzzle pieces belonging to their group and race to "reunite" the pieces to make the picture.*

In that game you had to bringing the pieces back together, and you ended up with a picture of people coming back together. We're going to carry on thinking about reunions now.

👂 Let's Hear from God

We began our Bible story in the first book of the Bible: Genesis. We thought about what life was like for Adam and Eve in the first garden. And we're going to finish our story in the last book of the Bible: Revelation. We're going to think about what life will be like for Jesus' friends in the last garden—a garden-city.

God gave one of Jesus' friends, John, a sneak preview of how the story of the whole world will end. This will happen when Jesus comes back and his friends live with him for ever. John wrote down for us what he saw. He described seeing a new heaven and a new earth that had gates and a wall and foundations and streets like a city.

Let's find out what else he saw:

⬇ For Younger Children

> ⓘ *Display the pictures provided for this session from The Garden, the Curtain and the Cross storybook (three different images: one imagining Eden, one imagining God's presence there with Adam and Eve, and one showing sin in the world). You'll use them to help the children to spot similarities and differences between what they have seen about Eden in Genesis and what they hear about Revelation. Use sticky notes to cover up (and so "remove") images showing anything that won't be present in the new creation—the tree of the knowledge of good and evil, sinful behaviours and sadness.)*

I'm going to read out some of the things that John was shown will happen when Jesus comes back and his friends get to live with him for ever. When you hear something that reminds you of anything in these pictures, I want you to point to the picture.

Revelation 22 v 1-2 says, "The angel showed [John] the river of the water of life. The river was shining like crystal. It flows from the throne of God and of the Lamb [that's Jesus] down the middle of the street of the city" (ICB).

- What can you see in these pictures of Eden that those verses remind you of?

God provided water to give life in Eden. God will give life in the new creation and life comes from the Lamb, who is Jesus.

Revelation 22 v 2 continues, "The tree of life was on each side of the river. It produces fruit 12 times a year, once each month. The leaves of the tree are for the healing of all people."

- What does that remind you of?

The tree of life means that people will live forever!

- What tree that was in Eden will NOT be in the new creation? *(Choose one of the two central trees on the Eden picture and cover it up.)*

There will be no sin in the new creation. No sin means no need to hide from God! Hurray!

Revelation 21 v 4 tells us that "[God] will wipe away every tear from their eyes. There will be no more death, sadness, crying, or pain. All the old ways are gone."

- Which pictures does that make you think of? *(Cover up all those pictures.)*

In the new creation, there will be nothing bad and no one sad! Imagine that!

In Revelation 21 v 3 John says, "I heard a loud voice from the throne. The voice said, 'Now God's home is with [people]. He will live with them, and they will be his people. God himself will be with them and will be their God.'"

- Which of these pictures imagines God living with people?

We can't imagine what that will look or be like, but Revelation 22 v 4 tells us that people "will see [God's] face". The bestest best thing of all about the new creation is that we will be able to see God and speak to God and just enjoy being with God. That's amazing!

> ⓘ *Now display this picture from The Garden, the Curtain and the Cross storybook, and give the children a moment to have a look at it:*

- This is a picture imagining the happy ending that Jesus has told us is waiting for his friends. Why do you think the people in the picture look so happy? *(Answers might include: because they get to be with God/Jesus; because there is nothing bad or sad; because they get to live for ever; because there is no more sin / their sin has been forgiven; because life there is great!)*

⬇ For Older Children

> ⓘ *If you use a Bible translation other than the ICB version, you may want to include Revelation 21 v 27 to enable the children to draw out the absence of sin and its effects in the new creation. In the ICB version, this can be drawn out from 22 v 3 more easily since "No longer will there be any curse" (NIV) is rendered as "Nothing that God judges guilty will be in that city".*

"¹ Then I saw a new heaven and a new earth. The first heaven and the first earth had disappeared. Now there was no sea. ² And I saw the holy city coming down out of heaven from God. This holy city is the new Jerusalem. It was prepared like a bride dressed for her husband. ³ I heard a loud voice from the throne. The voice said, 'Now God's home is with men. He will live with them, and they will be his people. God himself will be with them and will be their God. ⁴ He will wipe away every tear from their eyes. There will be no more death, sadness, crying, or pain. All the old ways are gone.'

⁵ The One who was sitting on the throne said, 'Look! I am making everything new!'"

(Revelation 21 v 1-5, ICB)

"¹ Then the angel showed me the river of the water of life. The river was shining like crystal. It flows from the throne of God and of the Lamb ² down the middle of the street of the city. The tree of life was on each side of the river. It produces fruit 12 times a year, once each month. The leaves of the tree are for the healing of all people. ³ Nothing that God judges guilty will be in that city. The throne of God and of the Lamb will be there. And God's servants will worship him. ⁴ They will see his face, and his name will be written on their foreheads. ⁵ There will never be night again. They will not need the light of a lamp or the light of the sun. The Lord God will give them light. And they will rule like kings forever and ever." (Revelation 22 v 1-5, ICB)

> ⓘ *Depending on time and your group, you could assign one or two particular categories from the list of five below to specific children or pairs of children. Revelation's imagery is complex—try not to get too bogged down in details!*

Read the two passages from Revelation 21 and 22. As you do, look out for anything that reminds you of the description of Eden in Genesis. Pick out verses that show us that life in the final garden-city will involve…

BEING IN THE GARDEN-CITY MEANS...	POSSIBLE ANSWERS/IDEAS
... perfect, unspoiled life	21 v 4-5: There will be nothing bad and no one sad; all the things that make life now hard—death, pain and so on—won't be there! Everything will be made new.
... perfect, unending life	22 v 2: The tree of life mentioned in Genesis is mentioned here too. It is for healing; it gives life. 22 v 5: The people will reign (and therefore live!) for ever and ever. (Children may also pick out "the river of the water of life" from 22 v 1, in which case it's worth noting with them what the source is—God and the Lamb, i.e. Christ.)
... perfect service of God	22 v 3: The people will serve and worship God.
... perfect, unending sinlessness	22 v 3: Nothing that God judges guilty will be there—that is, there will be no sin. OR "No longer will there be any curse": the curse on Adam and Eve and all humanity will be gone because sin has been dealt with and removed. (21 v 27: Only what is pure—sinless—will enter the city. Sin and its effects will not be there.) (21 v 1: Some children may have come across the idea that the sea represents evil and chaos, and will no longer be there. If they don't mention it, it may be better left, since it requires a lot of explaining and this point can be made without it.)
... the perfect, unlimited presence of God	21 v 3: This is a key verse, and it is worth spending time reading it aloud slowly and encouraging the children to reflect on how amazing that promise is. 22 v 4-5: God's people will see his face and enjoy their relationship with him (also emphasised by the bride-husband image of 21 v 2—see 19 v 7-8).

- What will God's people enjoy again, which was lost in Genesis 3? *(Possible answers: God being fully present with them; perfect relationships with God; perfect relationship with one another; eternal life; life without suffering; no death; no sin; not having to hide from God...)*
- Why is this ending of the story even better than enjoying having God live with us by his Holy Spirit now in this world?

What Does This Mean for Us?

God showed John the happy-ever-after ending that Jesus' friends can look forward to.

When we think about all the rescues and all the reunions we see in films, we can remember that Jesus rescued us from sin and death so that we will be reunited one day with God himself in his perfect place.

One day we will live with him in the place where there is nothing bad and no one sad, and we will be able to see God and speak to God and just enjoy being with God—just as he planned.

When we look forward to being in God's place, we most look forward to being reunited with him.

And in the meantime, while we wait, God is with us by his Holy Spirit. He helps us live as God's friends now and gets us ready for the day when we'll see him face to face.

> *Have a picture of a lightbulb or a WOW emoji, one of a speech bubble and another of a question mark. (The question mark is for using in the "Let's Talk To God about That" section.)*
>
> *Pointing to the lightbulb or WOW emoji…*

Take 30 seconds on your own in quiet to think about what has most interested or excited you from what you've learnt today.

- Now share it with a partner.
- Now let's share some of our thoughts as a whole group. *(Invite children to offer responses rather than picking on individuals. You could write up or draw their responses somewhere, ready for praying.)*

> *Pointing to the speech bubble…*

Take 30 seconds on your own in quiet to think about what you might like to say to God because of what we've learnt today.

- Now share it with a partner.
- Now let's share some of our thoughts as a whole group. *(Again, invite children to offer responses rather than picking on individuals. You could write up or draw their responses somewhere ready for praying.)*

Let's Talk to God about That

> *Here are a number of possible ways of encouraging the children to turn into prayer what they have learnt about God's presence with us now by his Spirit and eternally in the new creation. You will need to judge what is appropriate for your group. These ideas move loosely from most supported and least independent to most open and least scaffolded.*
>
> 1. *Pray on everyone's behalf, thanking God for his presence by his Spirit now and his eternal presence one day, and praising him for all the truths the children said excited or struck them in the course of the session. Close by asking God for the gift of faith to repent of sin and trust in Christ.*
>
> 2. *Tell the children that, as a group, you are going to praise God for who he is and thank him for what he has done and everything we can look forward to. Share these*

prayer sentence-starters, take a moment to recall some of the ideas you shared as a group in the discussion above, and then invite them to pray aloud if they want to finish off your sentences. Close by asking God for the gift of faith to repent of sin and trust in Christ:

- *Father God, we praise you because you are…*

- *Lord Jesus, thank you for…*

- *God with us, we thank you that one day…*

3. *Invite the children to enjoy a time of personal prayer or reflection. At this point you could give children who wish to the opportunity to think about any questions they have (see below).*

Pointing to the question mark…

If you have any questions about what we've learnt today or in any of the past weeks, you can either ask one of your leaders now as we enjoy [a craft/snack time] together or, if you prefer, you can write your name and your question on a piece of paper and put it in this box, and we will get an answer to you another time.

Let's Get Creative

Minimal resources:

- You'll need paper and coloured pens/pencils. Children can draw the scenes at Pentecost, or draw their own impression of some of what they have read about the new creation in Revelation, or draw what has most interested or excited them from the Bible's story of God's presence with his people.

Resources you may have available:

- You'll need the activity book accompanying *The Garden, the Curtain and the Cross*: the drawing page "Living with God".

- You'll need different colours of paper and some scissors. Show the children how to make paper chains of people (have plain paper if there will be time for them to draw and colour the people—otherwise lots of different colours of paper). Along where the hands join, children could write out words from Revelation 21 v 3: "He will live with them, and they will be his people. God himself will be with them and will be their God" (ICB).

- There are many free or cheap-to-purchase Bible-verse colouring pages available online. Search for one featuring a key verse from Revelation 21 v 1-5 or 22 v 1-5, or Matthew 28 v 20. Children can either colour it in or use it to help them design one of their own.

More of a project:

- Either individually or as a group use modelling putty on a card base to make a representation of life in the garden-city.

- Whole series project (see this section in Session 1 for more detail on this): For this session children can help add paper-chain people to a scene featuring the river and tree of life and a throne in the middle, or help make and/or decorate the throne itself to represent God's presence.

At Home

If you'd like to suggest ways that families could enjoy continuing to think about the lesson in the week:

- For younger children: They could read *The Garden, the Curtain and the Cross* storybook together. Perhaps they could have take-home questions along the lines of "When Jesus takes his friends to live with him, what will life be like there?" and/or "What can we say to Jesus now?"

- Suggest families watch one of the movies mentioned in the "Let's Get Ready" section on page 88 (where age-appropriate) and discuss the reunion that takes place at the end of the film and how it can remind us that God's people and God will live together again one day in God's place.

- Encourage children to learn a memory verse with their family or carer that gives us a picture of how wonderful it will be to live with God, such as some or all of…

    "God's dwelling-place is now among the people, and he will dwell with them.
    They will be his people, and God himself will be with them and be their God.
    'He will wipe every tear from their eyes. There will be no more death' or mourning
    or crying or pain, for the old order of things has passed away."
    (Revelation 21 v 3-4, NIV)

Tricky Questions

Children have a wonderful habit of asking great, and tricky, questions! Below are some of the questions or responses we anticipate these sessions may prompt, and suggested ways of answering them. These answers are aimed at 8-12-year-olds. Younger children will likely need slightly simpler answers!

All Bible quotations are from the NIV.

Session 1

Questions about how old the world is, whether God created it in six 24-hour days, and so on.

Christians don't all agree on exactly what Genesis 1 and 2 tell us about when and how the world was made. (Your church may well have its own position on this, in which case, of course, communicate that to the children.) But what is absolutely plain is this: this world was made by a Creator, who rules it; that men and women were made as part of the creation; and that the human race is unique because we are made in God's image, to relate to him and enjoy knowing him, to reflect what he's like to each other, and to rule creation under him. The Bible says in Genesis 1:27-28 that "God created mankind in his own image … [God said] 'Rule over the fish in the sea and the birds in the sky and over every living creature that moves on the ground.'"

It is good to think hard about what else the Bible is telling us about how God created everything, but it is also good to remember that these are the central truths of Genesis 1 – 2, and truths that all Christians understand and enjoy, even when they differ over other things.

Session 2

Who is Satan? Where did Satan come from? Why did God let him into the garden?

Satan is a fallen angel (angels being created spiritual beings who serve God in heaven and also act as his messengers)—it appears that he rebelled against God and so was thrown out of heaven, down to earth (Luke 10 v 18; Revelation 12 v 9). The Bible does not tell us a great deal about him, though it does want to warn us that he is real, he hates God, and his main aim is to stop people from loving and obeying God. It also wants to encourage us that Satan has been defeated by Jesus—because Jesus has made it possible for us to be forgiven for our sins, and because God's Spirit helps us to obey God, Satan has no power over Jesus' friends. One day, God will make it so that Satan is unable to do anything at all to tempt or harm God's people, ever again (Revelation 20 v 10).

The Bible does not tell us why God let Satan into the garden, or why he took the form of a snake (or, in some Bible translations, a serpent). That's probably because it wants us to focus on the humans—the creatures who are like us—and their actions when they were tempted.

Why did God let Adam and Eve disobey? Why did God create Adam and Eve if he knew they would disobey?

It is hard to get our heads round the way that God knows everything before it happens—and so thinking about questions like these can make our brain feel a bit stretched!

But there are two things we can say: firstly, God wanted the first humans to choose to be in friendship with him and to love him, and that meant they also had the choice to not love him and reject being friends with him. He could have made them in such a way that they had to obey him—but that would not have been a real friendship or real love.

Secondly, God is three Persons and one God—

Father, Son and Spirit. (This is often called the Trinity—another truth about God that can make our brain feel a bit stretched!) The Father, the Spirit and the Son all love each other and love to bring praise to each other. So God the Father loves to bring praise to God the Son, because the Son is wonderful. Because humans sinned, the Father sent the Son to die for us, so that we could be forgiven and live for ever with him, even though we don't deserve it. And that means we'll spend eternity praising God the Son, Jesus, and saying, "Thank you, Jesus. You're amazing!" in a way that we wouldn't have if Jesus hadn't ever needed to come and die for us. The Bible, in Revelation 5 v 12, tells us that in heaven this song is being sung: "Worthy is the Lamb [that's Jesus], who was slain, to receive power and wealth and wisdom and strength and honour and glory and praise!"

So the way things did turn out means that Jesus gets more praise from people who know that he died for them—and, because he's wonderful, that's a very good thing!

I don't think I'm sinful.

We need to be quite careful about saying that we don't sin, or that our sin doesn't matter—because then we are saying that we know better than God. This is God's world, and he knows everything about it and about us. And in the Bible he says, in 1 John 1 v 8, that "if we claim to be without sin, we deceive ourselves". And that is not a good idea, because if we think we don't sin, then we won't think we're in trouble and need God's forgiveness, and so we'll never ask Jesus to forgive us.

Jesus tells us in Mark 2 v 17 that to think we are not sinful—that we are "righteous"—is like a very sick person thinking they are not ill and don't need a doctor's help. The truth is that they do need healing, but they won't be healed because they don't think they need help. So it is with us—we need to accept that we sin. Then we are able to accept the help that Jesus offers us, because he came to rescue us from the consequences of our sin.

Here's another way to think about it. Among lots of other things, God tells you in the Bible not to be selfish, not to lie, not to steal, not to envy others, always to be kind… He says that to disobey him in these ways is to sin. Try living until this time tomorrow without putting yourself first in any way, without lying or stealing or envying, without being unkind in any way. I think you'll find you can't! That's because we are all, in fact, sinful. And that should make us sad. But it also brings us to a place where we can know great joy, because we know Jesus came to help sinners.

Session 3

The goat died for the people, but they still died eventually, right?

Yes, they did—just as we will, even if we are trusting that Jesus died for us. But the goat's death meant that they could carry on living as part of God's people, near to his presence in the tabernacle; and by trusting in the goat's death in their place, the people showed that they were trusting in God's promises to send someone to sort out all of the problems of sin and death. This kind of trust, or belief, is what meant someone was friends with God (James 2 v 23) and would therefore live for ever with him, after their death. That's the same for us, if you think about it—trusting in Jesus, who was the someone God sent to sort out the problem of sin and death by dying in our place, does not mean we will never die. It does mean that we are friends with God, and we can look forward to living for ever with him after we've died.

Aren't the sacrifices really unfair on/cruel to the goat who died?

It would be if the goat had been killed by the people just for fun. But God has given us animals for lots of different reasons, and one of them is so that the goats could be a picture of the truth that people deserve death because they sin but that God provides something else to die in their place. It's worth remembering that goats don't have thoughts and feelings in the same way as humans do, and they're not made in God's image. So while it's not ok to hurt or kill a goat just because you feel like it, it was ok for those people to make those sacrifices because God told them to.

How can blood make something clean?

Because we are not talking about being physically clean—like when you're muddy and you need water and soap to clean your skin. We're talking about being spiritually clean. Because the goat died in the place of the sinful people, the goat's death took away their sin—which we might think of as their spiritual dirt—so that they were clean. This is why God said, in Leviticus 16 v 30, that the sacrifice, the atonement, "will be made for you, to cleanse you. Then, before the Lord, you will be clean from all your sins". That's why we can say that blood can make someone clean. It's still the same today. We are washed clean of our sin because of the greatest sacrifice of all—Jesus' death for us. Hebrews 9 v 14 tells us that "the blood of Christ … [will] cleanse our consciences from acts that lead to death, so that we may serve the living God".

Session 4

How can God be a man? Are God the Father and God the Son different? Was Jesus really God?

Well, these are big questions! We're talking about what God is like, and our human minds can't understand all—or even most—of what God is like, because God is much more amazing than us! But what we can understand is what God reveals about himself in his Bible. God is one God, in three Persons. Each Person is fully God, and different from the other Persons. We tend to call the three Persons of the one God the Father, the Son (or Jesus), and the Spirit. Normally, 1+1+1 = 3. With God, it's different: 1+1+1 = 1. That makes our brains feels stretched! But that's ok—we just need to remember that there is one God (not three) and that within the one God there are three Persons—each fully God, each different from the others. So Jesus is God the Son, living on earth as a human. The Bible says that Jesus was "in very nature God … [and] made himself nothing by taking the very nature of a servant, being made in human likeness" (Philippians 2 v 6-7). God the Father and God the Son are both God, but they're not the same Person, which is why, when we read a Gospel, we see God the Son talking to, and talking about, his Father.

We don't fully understand how Jesus was God and a man. But we can see that he was, because he did things only God can do (calming a storm, raising people from the dead) and did things that real humans do (ate food, got tired, got thirsty, and so on). So when we look at Jesus, we are not seeing someone who is half-God, half-man (but not fully either). We're not seeing a human body with a God-mind. We're seeing someone who is fully God and fully man, at the same time, all the time. How does that work? We don't know for sure. We can see that it's true, without always understanding exactly how. But of course God can do things that we can't get our heads round. That's exciting!

If Jesus didn't sin then it wasn't fair that he died, was it?

In the way that we think about fairness, no, it wasn't fair! That's why it's amazing—God the Son chose to come and live on earth as a human, and then chose to die as a human, even though he didn't deserve it—because he knew that that was the way that he could take our sins and forgive us so that we could enjoy living with him for ever. If he'd said, "I'll only do what's fair", he would have stayed living in heaven, and we would not be able to enter heaven. But instead he said, "I'll do what's loving", and died on the cross for us. This is what Christians often call "grace"—Jesus died even though he didn't deserve to, to take our sins, so that we could live with him for ever even though we don't deserve to.

Session 5

Did Jesus really rise from the dead?

(For children aged 8 and up who enjoy reading, a great book about this is Chris Morphew's *How Do We Know That Christianity Is Really True?* published by The Good Book Company, 2021.)

There are lots of reasons why we can be confident that Jesus really rose from the dead:

- His tomb was empty and his body had gone—even Jesus' enemies didn't argue that it hadn't!

- It's very unlikely that his body had been stolen by robbers because his clothes—the only valuable things in the tomb—had been left behind (John 20 v 3-7).

- It's impossible that soldiers had moved the body because if they had, they'd have shown everyone the body when Jesus' friends, like Peter, started saying that Jesus had risen.

- The disciples had been terrified and defeated. Just over a month later, they were full of courage and joy. What made such a difference? It was seeing Jesus risen from the dead!

- The disciples said they had seen Jesus alive after he died, and that lots of other people—hundreds—had seen him too. In the next 30 years or so, most of the disciples died because of that claim. Would they all really have died for something they knew they had made up? Isn't it far more likely that they were willing to die for saying it because they knew it was true?

All these help us to believe Jesus really rose from the dead. But there's one more really great reason to believe, and it's this: Jesus rising from the dead shouldn't be a surprise—if he's God. In fact, if Jesus is God, then we should expect him to do things that no other human can do and that no other human can explain. Things like… rising from the dead! Jesus had promised several times that he would rise from death (for example, Mark 8 v 31 and 9 v 31). He had said that he was God, living on earth as a human (for instance, John 5 v 16-18). And so the resurrection is him proving who he is and keeping his promises. When we think about who Jesus is and what he'd said would happen, it would be far more shocking if he hadn't risen from the dead!

What happens to people who don't repent and believe?

If someone chooses not to repent and believe, then they're choosing not to live in friendship with God. That means they can't enjoy having God living in them by his Spirit now, and they can't enjoy living in God's presence for ever, beyond death. Instead, they still face God's judgment on their sin; remember, he says to humans, *Because of your sin, you can't come in*. There is a place beyond death, outside God's loving presence, where there's nothing good and everyone is always sad. The Bible's name for that place is hell. Jesus described hell in Mark 9 v 48 as a place where "the fire is not quenched" and in Luke 13 v 28 as a place of "weeping"—it is an awful place. It's very sad that people end up there.

So what should we do? Well, we should repent and believe ourselves, so that we can know that we have God's Spirit now and will live with him, in his perfect place, for ever. And we should tell other people how they can live with God too: by repenting and treating Jesus as King, and believing that Jesus has died so they can be forgiven.

Session 6

God just seems to have put things back to how they were at the start. Why go through all that?! Why not just make it so that Adam and Eve wouldn't sin in the first place?

Well, things are better at the end than the beginning! Firstly, there's a lot more people there. Secondly, the city of God's presence with his people fills the whole world, which is what Revelation 21 v 15-15-17 means, though it says it in a very complicated way! Thirdly, there is no longer any chance of things going wrong. Revelation 22 v 2 says that near the middle of the forever city "stood the tree of life", as in the Garden of Eden, but it does not mention the tree of the knowledge of good and evil because it's not there. That is telling us that all the humans who live there will have chosen Jesus is their King, and there's no chance of anyone sinning ever again. Fourthly, we get to praise Jesus for saving us. Jesus is wonderful, and he will get praise as our Saviour for ever, which he did not get in the Garden of Eden because he hadn't saved anyone then! So that's one big reason why God didn't make it so that Adam and Eve wouldn't sin in the first place.

What is so good about living for ever? Will worshipping God for ever really be very exciting?

Imagine the best day ever. Then imagine it's even better than that. Then imagine that it's even better than that. Perhaps you're coming close to how great it will be to be the perfect version of you, to enjoy a body that never goes wrong, and to live in the perfect place of God's presence. And then imagine that the next day is just as good, or even better—and you know that the amazingness is never, ever going to stop. That's eternity in God's presence.

One reason why we don't think worshipping God all the time sounds very exciting is because we're sinful, and so we think other things are more fun. When we're in God's forever place, we won't have sinful hearts anymore, and so we'll enjoy most of all the thing we were created to enjoy most of all—spending time with God. But there's another thing to think about: in the Garden of Eden, Adam worshipped God not only by praising him but by enjoying the place he'd given him and the people he'd put there. Adam worshipped by doing his job of looking after the garden and the animals. He worshipped by enjoying his relationship with Eve. He worshipped by enjoying the fruit from the trees. So when we think about worshipping God for ever, here is what that means. We will have a perfect job to do, and we'll worship God by doing it in the way he'd like and by saying, "Thank you for this job, God—you're amazing". And we will have perfect friendships, and we'll worship God by being a great friend and saying, "Thank you for my friends and for this chance to love them and enjoy them, God—you're amazing". And we will eat with Jesus and sing songs of praise around his throne—songs like the one in Revelation 5 v 12, which says, "Worthy is the Lamb [Jesus], who was slain, to receive power and wealth and wisdom and strength and honour and glory and praise". Which is a great way to say, "Thank you, Jesus—you're amazing!"

Meet the Rest of the Family

The Storybook

Specially Discounted Ministry Packs

You can buy ministry packs of all these resources at special discounts to enable you to give them to children at your church.

Head to the downloadable resources page and enter your passcode (see page 5) to find out more:

www.thegoodbook.com/gcclessonresources

Easter Calendar and Family Devotional

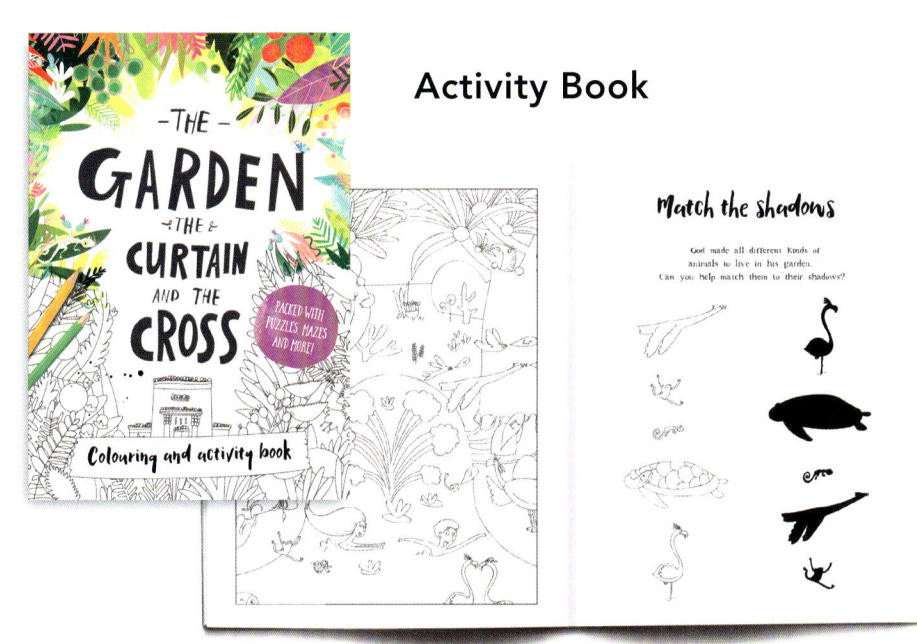

Activity Book

Board Book

thegoodbook
COMPANY

BIBLICAL | RELEVANT | ACCESSIBLE

At The Good Book Company, we are dedicated to helping Christians and local churches grow. We believe that God's growth process always starts with hearing clearly what he has said to us through his timeless word—the Bible.

Ever since we opened our doors in 1991, we have been striving to produce Bible-based resources that bring glory to God. We have grown to become an international provider of user-friendly resources to the Christian community, with believers of all backgrounds and denominations using our books, Bible studies, devotionals, evangelistic resources, and DVD-based courses.

We want to equip ordinary Christians to live for Christ day by day, and churches to grow in their knowledge of God, their love for one another, and the effectiveness of their outreach.

Call us for a discussion of your needs or visit one of our local websites for more information on the resources and services we provide.

Your friends at The Good Book Company

thegoodbook.com | thegoodbook.co.uk
thegoodbook.com.au | thegoodbook.co.nz
thegoodbook.co.in